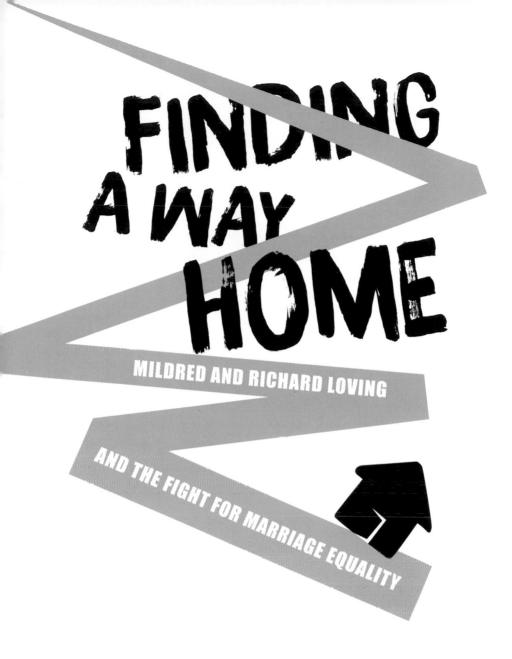

FINDING A WAY HOME

MILDRED AND RICHARD LOVING

AND THE FIGHT FOR MARRIAGE EQUALITY

LARRY DANE BRIMNER

CALKINS CREEK

AN IMPRINT OF BOYDS MILLS & KANE

New York

For Barbara Grzeslo,
who brings design creativity to the page

"All persons born or naturalized in the United States, and subject to the jurisdiction thereof, are citizens of the United States and of the State wherein they reside. No State shall make or enforce any law which shall abridge the privileges or immunities of citizens of the United States; nor shall any State deprive any person of life, liberty, or property, without due process of law; nor deny to any person within its jurisdiction the equal protection of the laws."

—US Constitution,
Fourteenth Amendment,
Section 1

"Almighty God created the races

white, black, yellow, malay and red,

and he placed them on separate

continents. . . . The fact that he

separated the races shows that he

did not intend for the races to mix."

—Judge Leon M. Bazile

January 22, 1965

Richard and Mildred Loving at home in Central Point, Virginia. Also seen are Richard's mother, Lola, and the couple's daughter, Peggy.

CONTENTS

Richard and Mildred Loving, husband and wife, lay in bed, sleeping, that warm, peaceful Virginia night in July 1958. Around 2:00 a.m., the stillness was shattered when they were jolted awake by the glare of three flashlights and rousted out of bed by Sheriff Garnett Brooks and two deputies. It was a show of force by the entire sheriff's department. The sheriff and his deputies had been to the house before, during daylight hours, but had never found anyone home. This surprise, middle-of-the-night raid rewarded the sheriff with the lawbreakers he had been seeking. Standing beside the bed, Sheriff Brooks demanded to know what Richard was doing with the woman.

A quiet man, no doubt confused by the intrusion, Richard didn't immediately answer the sheriff's question. Mildred spoke up instead, saying, "I'm his wife."

Sheriff Brooks fired back: "Not here you're not." Richard pointed to the couple's marriage license that the newlyweds had hung on the bedroom wall, as if to prove Mildred's words were indeed fact, but the sheriff scoffed, saying, "That's no good here."

Richard, a twenty-four-year-old bricklayer, and Mildred, a housewife just shy of her nineteenth birthday, had known each other most of their lives. He was white. She was "colored—part [American] Indian and part Negro." Lifelong residents of Virginia, they lived in Central Point, a small rural area in Caroline County some fifty miles northeast of Richmond, the state capital.

Mixed marriages—those between a white person and a member of any other race—were against the custom in Virginia. They were also against the law. It had been that way ever since colonial times. Richard and Mildred had committed the crime of falling in love and marrying while continuing to live near their families and friends in Virginia.

The sheriff charged the young couple with unlawful cohabitation—living together and having sexual relations without benefit of marriage—and arrested them. As Mildred remembered, Sheriff Brooks and his deputies then "carried us to Bowling Green and locked us up." Bowling Green is where Caroline County's seat of government is located.

While separation of the races in Virginia was commonplace, in Central Point it was different. The rural world in which Mildred Delores Jeter and Richard Perry Loving grew up in the 1950s wasn't strictly divided racially into white and black. It was both segregated and interlaced. "It never was like a lot of other places," Richard recalled later. "It [race] doesn't matter to folks around here. They just want to live and be left alone." The couple had attended racially divided schools and churches, but in other ways, the races mixed. Richard's mother, Lola Loving, was a midwife and delivered most of the babies in the area, black or white. Richard often stopped by the Jeter household to listen to Mildred's seven brothers play what Mildred called "hillbilly music" and to talk about race cars. He and two black friends owned a car together and raced it *Text continued on page 14*

Mildred Dolores Jeter and Richard Perry Loving had known each other most of their lives and married in 1958 despite Virginia's prohibition against mixed-race marriages. She was African American; he was Caucasian, or of white European ancestry. When they married, they did not know it would lead to their arrests and years of legal battles for the right to live in Virginia as husband and wife.

STATE OF VIRGINIA,

County of Caroline } **To-wit:**   Commonwealth Warrant

To the Sheriff or any Police Officer of the said County:

WHEREAS, *Bernard Mahon Connally* of the said County, has this day made complaint and information on oath before me, Robert W. Farmer, Justice of the Peace of the said County

that *Richard Loving (a white person) and Peter Jeter (a colored)*

in the said County did on the *2nd* day of *June*, 19*58*,

unlawfully and feloniously *did go out of this State for the purpose of being married and with the intention of returning and were married out of state, and afterwards, returned to and resided in it, cohabiting as man & wife*

against the peace and dignity of the Commonwealth of Virginia.

These are, Therefore, to command you, in the name of the Commonwealth, to apprehend and bring before the Judge of the said County the body of the said *Richard Loving & Jeter*

to answer the said complaint, and to be further dealt with according to law. And you are directed to summon _____

mon _____

_____ as witnesses.

Given under my hand and seal this *11th* day of *July*, 19*58*

Robert W. Farmer, J. P.

STATE OF VIRGINIA   **To-wit:**

County of Caroline _____

I, *J. L. Webb*, Justice of the Peace in and for the County aforesaid, State

of Virginia, do certify that *Richard Loving* and

Eleanor A. & John Koons, by, Robert E. Buchan, as his

attorney in fact

suret _____, have this day acknowledged themselves indebted to the Commonwealth of Virginia in the

sum of *One thousand no/100* Dollars ($*1,000*),

to be made and levied of their respective goods and chattels, upon this condition: That the said _____

Richard Loving shall appear before the

~~Circuit~~ County Court of the said County, on the *17th* day of *July*

19*58*, at *10* A. M., at *Bowling Green*, Va., and not leave hence without the leave of the said Court, and that he appears before the Court to answer the charge in this warrant, and/or any continuance thereof, and/or abide the judgment of said Court, and/or any appeal therefrom, or to await the action of the Grand Jury upon the within charge, at such time or times as may be prescribed by the Court and at any time or times to which the proceedings may be continued or further heard, and to remain in full force and effect until the charge is finally disposed of or until it is declared void by order of a competent Court.

Given under my hand, this *14th* day of *July*, 19*58*

J. L. Webb, J. P.

The following witnesses were recognized to appear before the

Circuit
County Court of Caroline County, Virginia, at Bowling Green, Virginia,
at .... M. on the ....
day of ...., 19.., ,
under penalty of $ ....

....
....
....
....
....
....
....
....
....
....
....
....
....

7/17-58

Mile 42-21

Criminal Docket No. ...*928*....

COMMONWEALTH
vs. { WARRANT OF ARREST

Richard Loving

Executed this, the *13th* day
of *July*, 19*58*
Garnett Brooks Sh.

Upon the defendant's plea of ....
Not guilty to the within
charge, and upon examination of the
witnesses, I find ~~the accused~~ *probable
cause to charge the accused
with a felony and it
is ordered that he be held
for the action of the Grand
Jury 7-17-58*

Leonard ..... Judge

Fine ..... $ ....
Costs ..... $ ....

Total ..... $ ....

COSTS:

Fine	$	
Warrant	$	*1.50*
County Judge	$	*2.00*
Clerk	$	*1.25*
Arrest	$	*1.00*
Mileage	$	*5.04*
Summoning Witness .	$	
Witness' Attendance .	$	
Jail Fee	$	*.50*
Commonwealth Attorney	$	*2.50*
Bail Fee	$	
	$	
Circuit Court Cost	$	*22.50*
Total	$	*36.29*
Witness		
	$	
	$	
	$	
	$	
	$	
	$	
	$	
	$	

Richard's arrest warrant states that he had broken the law because he, as a white person, left the state of Virginia to marry someone of a different race and then returned to it to live, an attempt to evade the statutes against mixed marriages. Note his initial plea of "not guilty" and the costs involved in the arrest.

Sheriff Garnett Brooks was doing his job when he arrested Richard and Mildred, but according to people who knew him, he did not like African Americans and was deeply offended by mixed-race marriages. When asked if Brooks was a racist, a member of Richard's drag racing team responded, "Hell, yes."

most weekends, often winning against local rivals. But eventually, Mildred—nicknamed String Bean, for her tall, slender figure and which Richard shortened to Bean—became his reason to visit. For Mildred, however, it wasn't love at first sight. "When we first met," she recalled, "I didn't like him. . . . But I got to know him and he was a very nice person."

At the time, the South was still grappling with an American society that had begun to change after World War II. Both whites and blacks had fought in that war, but black soldiers returned home to inequality and segregation. Many thought that this treatment wasn't right, and it began to show itself in the arts, and also in the courts. But the South was different, frozen in a past time. It fought to preserve its old ways.

In 1953, two Georgia legislators, Representative David C. Jones and Senator John D. Shepard, had criticized the popular stage musical of the day, *South Pacific*, for its portrayal of interracial romantic relationships. Specifically, the two men were offended by one song's lyrics: "You've got to be taught to be afraid of people whose . . . skin is a diff'rent shade." According to Jones, the song was offensive. "Intermarriage," he said, "produces halfbreeds. And halfbreeds are not conducive to the higher type of society. We in the South are a proud and progressive people. Halfbreeds cannot be proud." He went on to say, incorrectly, the people in the South have "pure blood lines and we intend to keep it that way."

In Virginia, white state legislators fought the postwar attitudes by strictly enforcing racial integrity statutes—laws meant to preserve the purity of the white race—which dictated who a person could and could not marry. These legislators also defied the United States Supreme Court's 1954 decision in *Brown v. Board of Education* that said segregated schools were unlawful, fearful that integrated schools would lead to mixed, or interracial, marriages. Virginia wasn't alone in its fear and defiance;

RODGERS & HAMMERSTEIN'S

SOUTH PACIFIC

COLOR by DE LUXE

— ROSSANO BRAZZI • MITZI GAYNOR • JOHN KERR • FRANCE NUYEN

BUDDY ADLER — JOSHUA LOGAN

South Pacific was a popular post WWII stage musical and, later, movie that took on the issue of interracial relationships. When asked what he thought about the Georgia legislators' negative reaction to his work, Oscar Hammerstein II, co-creator of the musical, said he doubted he would have anything in common with them.

all of the Southern states that made up the former Confederate States of America refused to recognize the *Brown* ruling. Adding to the South's distress was the yearlong bus boycott in Montgomery, Alabama, after Rosa Parks's 1955 arrest for disregarding Alabama's bus-seating policies. These ordinances required black people to sit at the back of the bus and to give up their seat if told to move by a white person. In a case known as *Browder v. Gayle* the following year, the Supreme Court struck down these Jim Crow laws. Jim Crow was the name commonly given to policies that separated people by race. Nonetheless, despite signs that the US was becoming more just, the South tended to ignore the Supreme Court's rulings regarding racial equality. And so it was in Virginia. But, somewhat naive and sheltered by the easygoing attitudes about race in Central Point, Richard and Mildred had begun dating.

Before long, Mildred discovered she was pregnant, and the couple decided they wanted to become husband and wife. Mildred, who had an infant from a previous relationship, was unaware that in Virginia it was illegal for them to wed. "I didn't know it was against any law," Mildred explained later. "We were just happy to be together." Richard, however, knew there was some sort of Jim Crow prohibition to them marrying in Virginia, but he didn't know the full extent of that law. He decided they should go to Washington, DC, where it was legal for mixed-race couples to marry. "We weren't out to change nothing," Mildred said, when she was interviewed in 1992. They were just a couple who wanted to demonstrate their love by marrying.

They made two trips to Washington, the first on May 24, 1958, to get a marriage license. On Monday, June 2, they returned with Mildred's father and brother Otho, who would act as witnesses to the marriage and keep them company. Since they didn't know any preachers, they

No. 420276

Marriage License

To Reverend __John L. Henry__

authorized to celebrate marriages in the District of Columbia, GREETING:

You are hereby authorized to celebrate the rites of marriage between

__Richard Perry Loving__ , of __Passing, Virginia__

AND

__Mildred Delores Jeter__ , of __Passing, Virginia__

and having done so, you are commanded to make return of the same to the Clerk's Office of the United States District Court for the District of Columbia within TEN days, under a penalty of $50 for default therein.

WITNESS my hand and seal of said Court, this __2nd__

day of __June__ , anno Domini 19 __58__

HARRY M. HULL, Clerk.

By __Maud K Rynex__

Deputy Clerk

No. 420276

Return

I, Reverend __John L. Henry__

who have been duly authorized to celebrate the rites of marriage in the District of Columbia, do hereby certify that, by authority of license of corresponding number herewith, I solemnized the marriage of

__Richard Perry Loving__ and __Mildred Delores Jeter__

named therein, on the __2nd__ day of __June__ , 19 __58__ , at __748 Princeton Place, N. W.__

(Name of church, or street address, etc.)

in said District.

6/4/58 ✓ ewg

FPI ERO—8-19-57-10M-7208

__Rev. John L. Henry__

The Washington, DC, marriage license that Richard and Mildred had hung on their bedroom wall as a testament of their love. The license incorrectly lists their place of residence as Passing, Virginia. They lived in Central Point on Passing Road.

chose one from a phone book—a Reverend John L. Henry—to perform the ceremony. The foursome returned to Caroline County, but this time Richard and Mildred were husband and wife, at least in Washington, DC. Until the young couple could afford for Richard to build them a house of their own, they lived with Mildred's parents, occupying the downstairs bedroom, while Theoliver and Musiel, her father and mother, slept in a bedroom upstairs.

The newlyweds lived undisturbed in the Jeter home for a while. At first, no one in the tightly knit community of Central Point seemed to pay any attention or voice any concerns or objections. "But we had one enemy, I guess," Mildred recalled. Someone filed an anonymous tip with Bernard Mahon, the politically ambitious county prosecutor, and on July 11, Robert W. Farmer, a justice of the peace, acted on Mahon's complaint that a white man and a Negro woman "did go out of this State [Virginia] for the purpose of being married . . . and with the intention of returning." Richard and Mildred had broken Virginia's law by leaving the state to marry, and then returning to live "as man and wife." Farmer issued arrest warrants for the couple on July 11. A few days later, on July 14, Sheriff Brooks and his deputies arrested the pair during the 2:00 a.m. raid and took them to the Bowling Green jail.

Bowling Green's two-story jail, erected in 1902, was meant for serious detention. It was built of steel, with red brick covering the exterior. Male prisoners were housed in a cell downstairs. Upstairs, there was another lockup for people arrested for public drunkenness, along with a small room at the top of the stairs, with one bunk and a single toilet, for one female or juvenile prisoner at a time. Iron bars in a checkerboard pattern covered this room's door and window. Richard was held downstairs, but his sister arranged for him to be released on bail the next day. Mildred, however, was detained in the little rodent-infested cell upstairs for several days more, and Richard understood that if he or anyone else tried to get her released, he would be rearrested. He was helpless to protect his wife.

Mere days before the grand jury was to meet on October 13, Donald Loving was born on October 8. Since their release from the Bowling Green jail, the couple had lived apart, Richard with his parents and Mildred with hers. Nevertheless, Richard's mother delivered Donald, just as she had Mildred's firstborn, Sidney, in January 1957.

After the Caroline County grand jury met, forewoman Gladys Livermon signed a formal indictment against the couple. It charged that "Richard Perry Loving being a White person and . . . Mildred Delores Jeter being a Colored person, did unlawfully and feloniously go out of the State of Virginia, for the purpose of being married, and with the intention of returning to the State of Virginia . . . against the peace and dignity of the Commonwealth." A grand jury's role isn't to determine guilt or innocence, but rather to decide whether there are reasonable grounds (probable cause) to bring those arrested for a crime to trial. On October 16, the weekly newspaper, the *Caroline Progress*, broke the news to the public: "The grand jury indicted Richard Perry Loving, alleged to be white, and Mildred Delores Jeter, alleged to be colored, for going out of the state and marrying and returning to the state to live, contrary to the state law against mixed marriages."

Virginia wasn't the only state to have such a statute in 1958. Twenty-four of the forty-eight states, including all the states that made up the South, outlawed marriage between races. This, in turn, led to most states defining whiteness as having no trace of non-white blood. Going back generations, a single drop of non-white blood made a person ineligible to marry a white person. While Richard had understood that they couldn't marry in Virginia, he had not known that it was against *Text continued on page 24*

Although no longer in use, the Caroline County jail facility in Bowling Green, Virginia, is built of red brick and steel. A large cell downstairs and another upstairs was for male prisoners. A small cubicle opposite the window above the door was where Mildred was held for several days after Richard had been released on bail.

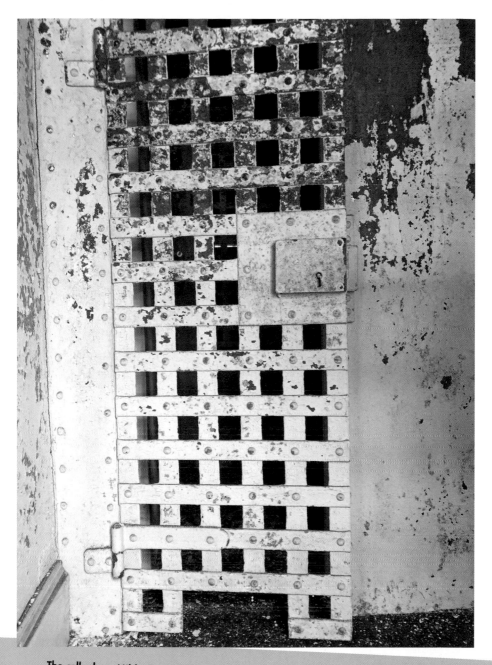

The cell where Mildred was held is as wide as the stairwell and accommodated only one prisoner at a time. The door is made of heavy steel, now rusted. Note the large opening at the bottom of the door; a tray of food would have been pushed through it at mealtime. One deputy, offended by the idea of interracial marriage, threatened Mildred by saying he might leave the door unlocked so that other prisoners could get to her. The threat terrified the young bride.

STATE OF VIRGINIA, } To-wit: Commonwealth Warrant
County of Caroline

To the Sheriff or any Police Officer of the said County:

WHEREAS, _Bernard Mahon Com. atty._ of the said County, has this day made complaint and information on oath before me, Robert W. Farmer, Justice of the Peace of the said County that ~~_____~~ _Mildred Jeter a negro_

in the said County did on the _2nd_ day of _June_ _____, 19_58_

unlawfully and feloniously _did go out of this State for the purpose of being married to a white person, and with the intention of returning, and was married out of State and afterwards returned to and resided in it Cohabiting as man & wife_

against the peace and dignity of the Commonwealth of Virginia.

These are, Therefore, to command you, in the name of the Commonwealth, to apprehend and bring before the Judge of the said County the body of the said _____

Mildred Jeter

to answer the said complaint, and to be further dealt with according to law. And you are directed to summon _____

_____ as witnesses.

Given under my hand and seal this _11th_ day of _July_ _____, 19_58_

Robert W. Farmer, J. P.

STATE OF VIRGINIA   To-wit:
County of Caroline _____

I, _Edward Stehl III_____, Justice of the Peace in and for the County aforesaid, State of Virginia, do certify that _Mildred Jeter_ _____ and

Rommie W. Catlett _____, as his

suret _y_ _____, have this day acknowledged themselves indebted to the Commonwealth of Virginia in the sum of _One Thousand_ _____ Dollars ($ _1,000.00_),

to be made and levied of their respective goods and chattels, upon this condition: That the said _____

Mildred Jeter _____ shall appear before the

~~Circuit~~
~~County~~ Court of the said County, on the _13th_ day of _October_

19_58_, at _10 00_ A/P. M., at _Bowling Green_ _____, Va., and not leave hence without the leave of the said Court, and that he appears before the Court to answer the charge in this warrant, and/or any continuance thereof, and/or abide the judgment of said Court, and/or any appeal therefrom, or to await the action of the Grand Jury upon the within charge, at such time or times as may be prescribed by the Court and at any time or times to which the proceedings may be continued or further heard, and to remain in full force and effect until the charge is finally disposed of or until it is declared void by order of a competent Court.

Given under my hand, this _24th_ day of _July_ _____, 19_58_

Rommie W. Catlett _Edward Stehl III_, J. P.

2

The following witnesses were re-cognized to appear before the

Circuit
County Court of Caroline County,
Virginia, at Bowling Green, Virginia,
at .... M. on the ....
day of ...., 19..,
under penalty of $ ....

....
....
....
....
....
....
....
....
....
....
....
....
....
....
....
....
....

Trial 7-17-58
Mile - 42-21

Criminal Docket No. ....929....

COMMONWEALTH
WARRANT OF ARREST

vs. {

Mildred Jeter

Executed this, the ....17.... day

of ....July...., 19*58*

Garnett Brooks, S

Upon the defendant's plea of ....

Not guilty .... to the within

charge, and upon examination of the

witnesses, I find ~~the accused~~ ....

*probable cause to charge
the accused with a felony
and it is ordered that she
be held for the action
of the Grand Jury 7-17-58*
*Edward Stephens
Judge*

Fine . . . . . $ ......

Costs . . . . . $ _____

Total . . . . . $ _____

Bond fee 7.00 pd 7-24-58

COSTS:

Fine . . . . $ ....
Warrant . . . . . $ *1.50*
County Judge . . . . $ *2.00*
Clerk . . . . $ *1.25*
Arrest . . . . . . $ *1.00*
Mileage . . . . . $ *5.04*
Summoning Witness . $ ....
Witness' Attendance . $ ....
Jail Fee . . . . . $ *.50*
Commonwealth Attorney $ *2.50*
Bail Fee *7-24-58* . $ *2.00*

Circuit Court Cost $ *22.50*

Total . . . . . . $ *36.29*
Witness

$ ....
$ ....
$ ....
$ ....
$ ....
$ ....
$ ....
$ ....
$ ....
$ ....

Because Virginia didn't recognize mixed-race marriages as valid, they didn't exist as far as the state was concerned. Therefore, state records referred to Mildred not as Loving, but her maiden name, Jeter.

the law for them to leave the state to get married and then to return to Virginia to live as husband and wife. But according to Virginia law, it was a felony, or serious crime, punishable by up to five years in state prison.

The couple's trial began on January 6, 1959, with circuit court judge Leon M. Bazile presiding. Although the couple had originally pleaded not guilty, on the advice of their attorney Frank Beazley, they did not dispute the facts of the case when they were laid out before them. Indeed, they had left the state to marry. They had returned to Virginia to live as husband and wife. After hearing the state law explained and the evidence against them, they changed their pleas to guilty and waived their right to a trial before a jury. The judge could have sentenced them to five years in the state penitentiary, but instead he fixed their punishment "at one year each in jail." He then immediately suspended their sentences "upon the provision that both accused leave Caroline County and the state of Virginia at once and do not return together or at the same time to said county and state for a period of twenty-five years." In other words, Richard Loving and Mildred Jeter, as they were known in the Virginia courts because the state didn't recognize their marriage, were forced to leave the state if they wanted to live as husband and wife. They were also not allowed to visit their families or friends, as any married couple might do, for a period of twenty-five years. If they attempted to come home together and were discovered by law enforcement, they could be rearrested and sent to jail for the one-year period set by the judge. As a couple, the Lovings had been banished.

2 — BANISHMENT

Almost immediately after their trial, the couple packed the few belongings they owned into Richard's car and left Virginia for Washington, DC, where they moved in with Mildred's cousin Alex Byrd and his wife, Laura. But neither Richard nor Mildred adapted to city life. Mildred especially missed the sights and sounds and smells of the country. She wanted her children to experience having grass beneath their bare feet and the freedom to roam. She complained that "the children didn't have anywhere to play. It was like being caged. And I couldn't stand it." She longed for her family. The couple realized they were not allowed to live in Virginia, but they were unclear about any other restrictions Judge Bazile had placed on them. From time to time, they returned to Virginia with the children to visit family and friends. Yet when they returned, they took care to avoid drawing attention to themselves, often staying in a neighboring county. During these visits, Richard usually remained indoors while Mildred visited with her parents or her sister Garnet.

In 1959, Easter fell in March. Richard and Mildred returned to Central

Point to spend the holiday with their families. But on March 28, the day before Easter Sunday, the sheriff rearrested them for violating their parole. He had received a tip that they were in the county. In Mildred's words, "That Easter we came back and they got us again." Judge Bazile ordered them to pay a $200 bond and to appear before the court in April. "The way I understood it," Mildred explained later, "the lawyer said that we could come back to visit . . . when we wanted to." Frank Beazley, the couple's lawyer, told the judge that it was his fault for misunderstanding the couple's parole terms. He said he had advised them that they could return together as long as they didn't stay in the same house overnight. This was not what Bazile's ruling had ordered, and it is quite possible that Beazley actually had understood the terms of the couple's parole. The two men had been friends for some time, and the judge accepted the lawyer's explanation. Bazile was lenient and dismissed the charges against the couple, sparing the Lovings from having to spend any more time in jail, but he cautioned them that he would not be so forgiving if they ever broke parole again.

"We left there and went to DC," Richard said, but life in Washington was never as happy as it had been in Caroline County before their arrests. Richard spent his days working at a construction job in northern Virginia. Mildred stayed at home with the two children and was miserable. "In Washington," Mildred lamented, "I just wanted to go back home."

Later that spring, Mildred became pregnant again. Despite the risks, she wanted to return to Caroline County so that Richard's mother could deliver the baby. Sometime in December, they went home, and the day after Christmas, Mildred's third child, Peggy, was born.

The couple continued to make their quiet visits to Virginia, but always with the risk of being caught, sent to jail, and separated from their children. Still, the bond with their families was strong, matched only by the pull to get home. As Peggy put it years later, "When they wanted to come back to Virginia for any reason, they're gonna come back together. They'll just take their chance." They lived like this, exiled, throughout 1960, 1961, and 1962. And except for their secretive trips to Virginia, they spent most of this time in Washington.

Neither Richard nor Mildred was political. Yet, throughout the country, black leaders and youthful organizers were calling for equal rights and constitutional justice. The US Supreme Court heard their calls. It had banned segregated seating on interstate buses (those that crossed state borders) in 1946. In 1954, it passed the *Brown* decision, which outlawed segregated schools. These decisions were ignored in the South and went unchallenged and unenforced, but still they were the laws of the land. In 1956, the court stepped in to end the yearlong Montgomery bus boycott when it ruled that racial seating on municipal buses also was illegal.

As a new decade dawned, the Supreme Court expanded its civil rights judgments to make segregated waiting areas and restaurants at bus terminals unlawful. The new decade also brought challenges to the South's traditions and customs in the form of sit-ins, which began when four black students sat down at a Woolworth's lunch counter in Greensboro, North Carolina, to take a stand against policies that denied them basic equality. Then in 1961, a mixed-race group of Freedom Riders boarded two buses in Washington, DC, determined to show that federal civil rights laws were being ignored. Mildred later commented on her connection to these protests and demonstrations, saying, "I wasn't involved in the civil rights movement. The only thing I know is what everybody saw on the [television] news." *Text continued on page 30*

27

In Montgomery, Alabama, 1961, unidentified Freedom Riders are protected by National Guard soldiers with bayonets affixed to their rifles.

The same was true for Richard. Central Point had sheltered the couple from the harsher realities of race relations beyond their rural world.

In 1963, television news programs practically crackled with black protesters demanding equality and white resistance to those demands. Images of threatening police dogs and of fire hoses being turned on young demonstrators in Birmingham, Alabama, hit the airwaves all across the United States and around the world in the spring of that year. In August 1963, a quarter million people of all races, genders, and religions marched on Washington to show their support for equal rights. They came by bus, by automobile, by train, and by plane for what was, at the time, the largest protest in the history of the United States. The Ku Klux Klan, a white supremacy group dedicated to keeping the races apart, found the March on Washington for Jobs and Freedom threatening to its mission. In September, its members exploded a dynamite bomb outside the Sixteenth Street Baptist Church in Birmingham, Alabama, to show their opposition to equality and school desegregation, killing four little black girls in the process.

Sometime in 1963, Sidney, the couple's oldest child, ran to tell his mother that Donald had been hit by a car. Mildred found Donald sitting on the sidewalk, uninjured but crying, and she later recalled, "That was the straw that broke the camel's back. I had to get out of there." She added, "I was so unhappy. I was complaining to my cousin constantly. So one Saturday, I guess she got tired of it. She told me, 'Write to Bobby Kennedy. That's what he's up there for.'" Robert F. "Bobby" Kennedy was the attorney general of the United States. His brother, President John F. Kennedy, had been trying to persuade Congress to pass a civil rights bill to quell the racial unrest in the nation, calling it a moral obligation to extend equality

The August 1963 March on Washington for Jobs and Freedom drew a quarter million people in peaceful protest for equal rights. The next month, on September 15, at the Sixteenth Street Baptist Church in Birmingham, Alabama, the Ku Klux Klan exploded a dynamite bomb that killed four little black girls. The Civil Rights Act of 1964, which banned discrimination in public places and outlawed inequality in the labor market, became law the following year.

1151 Neal St.
N.E. Wash. D.C.
June 20, 1963

Dear sir:

I am writing to you concerning a problem we have.

5 yrs. ago my husband and I were
married here in the District. We than returned
to Va. to live. My husband is White, I am part
negro, & part indian.

At the time we did not know there was
a law in Va. against mixed marriages.

Therefore we were jailed and tried in a
little town of Bowling Green.

We were to leave the state to make our home.

The problem is we are not allowed to visit
our families. The judge said if we enter the
state within the next 30 yrs., that we will
have to spend 1 yr. in jail.

We know we can't live there, but we
would like to go back once and awhile to
visit our families & friends.

We have 3 children and cannot afford
an attorney.

We wrote to The Attorney General, he
suggested that we get in touch with you.

for advice.
Please help us if you can. Hope to
hear from you real soon,
Yours Truely,
Mr. + Mrs. Richard Loving

Mildred wrote to Robert F. "Bobby" Kennedy after the Civil Rights Act of 1964 passed. She followed his advice and wrote the letter seen here to the American Civil Liberties Union to explain the couple's situation and ask for help.

to all of America's citizens. As head of the US Department of Justice, Robert Kennedy had been instrumental to seeing that federal laws were being enforced.

Mildred wrote to the attorney general. When Kennedy responded, he said "there wasn't anything he could do, but to write to the American Civil Liberties Union." On June 20, 1963, Mildred wrote to the American Civil Liberties Union (ACLU), a national organization that fights through the court system to defend the constitutional rights guaranteed to all individuals, and explained their situation: "Dear Sir:" her letter began. "5 yrs. ago my husband and I were married here in the District. We than [sic] returned to Va. to live. My husband is White, I am part negro, & part indian [sic]." After explaining that they had been jailed and were forbidden by the judge to visit their families under threat of more jail time, she said that she had written "to the Attorney General, [and] he suggested that we get in touch with you for advice."

The US Supreme Court had long skirted the issue

of marriage as a civil right. Cases that touched on interracial marriage had come before it, but the justices had never addressed the issue head on. The American Civil Liberties Union was eager for a test case to put before the court that would require it to rule on the constitutionality of state statutes that prohibited mixed marriages.

The ACLU forwarded Mildred's letter to Bernard S. Cohen, a young attorney who had earned his law degree in 1961 and who worked with the organization from his office in Alexandria, Virginia. Cohen found the circumstances of their case irresistible. This might be the case the ACLU had been looking for. Cohen believed the state laws against mixed-race marriages were, in his words, "relics of slavery . . . [meant] to keep the colored person down and the white person up." Despite Virginia's Racial Integrity Act of 1924, which made it illegal for a white person—defined as an individual having no non-white blood—to marry anyone other than another white person, the lawyer thought the subject of love and marriage should not rest with the state, but with the individuals involved.

"Marriage," he said later, "is a fundamental right of man."

Cohen was confident the Lovings had a constitutional problem that would make it to the US Supreme Court, if only he could figure out how to get it there. He also realized it would be "an unbelievable challenge for a lawyer one or two years out of law school to be getting involved in what was sure to be a major civil rights case." He arranged to meet the Lovings at an office he kept in the District of Columbia, so they would not have to break parole by driving into Virginia together. The couple may not have understood all the Fourteenth Amendment complexities that Cohen laid out before them, or that their case might actually end up before the justices of the Supreme Court, or how slowly the wheels of justice turn. But Cohen explained that the Fourteenth Amendment, under its due process and equal protection clauses, requires a state to apply its laws fairly to all citizens within its borders. He reasoned that Virginia's laws were in violation of the amendment because they were meant to protect only the purity of the white race. There were no equivalent laws to prevent individuals of any other race from marrying someone outside their racial group, as long as they were not attempting to marry a white person.

He also believed the twenty-five-year banishment was unreasonable and arbitrary, a clear violation of due process, or fairness. Cohen took a liking to Mildred and Richard almost immediately. Clearly the couple loved each other, and wanted to remain married. The lawyer viewed their love as an asset, but he realized he had a problem. He needed to get the couple's judgment back into the Virginia courts. Pleading guilty, which Mildred and Richard had done at their 1959 hearing, almost always eliminates any chance for appeal. Also, according to Virginia law, appeals in criminal cases had to be filed within sixty days of the verdict. That time had long since passed. Cohen had to figure out a way to overcome these obstacles. Text continued on page 38

35

The Lovings are seen here in Bernard S. Cohen's law office for a press interview. The couple seldom met with their attorneys to discuss the case.

Some months into his research, Cohen thought he might have found what he was looking for. He ran across a 1949 decision by the Virginia Supreme Court which had ruled that state law permitted a review of a case that involved a suspended sentence and probation, because it was "still in the breast of the court," or in its authority. Cohen believed the 1949 ruling could be applied to the Loving case.

On November 6, 1963, the ACLU lawyer filed a motion with Judge Bazile's court in Caroline County, requesting that the judge review the Loving case and set aside the couple's convictions and sentences. He argued that their "sentence constitutes cruel and unusual punishment" under the Virginia Constitution and that it "exceeds the reasonable period of suspension permitted." Among the several reasons Cohen listed to vacate the judgment, he included that the "sentence constitutes banishment, and is thus a violation of constitutional due process of law." He called the statute the couple's convictions were based upon—the mixed-race marriage prohibition—"unconstitutional on its face, in that it denies the defendants the equal protection of the laws and denies the right of marriage which is a fundamental right of free men." He also noted that "such sentence has worked undue hardship upon the defendants by preventing them from together visiting their families from time to time as may be desireable [sic] and necessary."

Judge Bazile responded to Cohen's motion with silence.

Seven months passed, and still Cohen had not heard whether the judge would reconsider the sentences he had handed down to Mildred and Richard in 1959. The lawyer took some comfort in knowing Bazile hadn't immediately rejected his motion, but he didn't know what more he could do to get the judge to act. For their part, the Lovings must have thought that Cohen had forgotten about them, because a little over a year

38

after she first had written to the ACLU, Mildred sent another letter, this one directly to Cohen. On July 6, 1964, she wrote to ask if he remembered them and expressed hope that the Civil Rights Act of 1964, which had just been passed on July 2, and which prohibited job discrimination and segregation in public places, might offer them relief. "Can they really stop us from visiting Va?" she asked. Cohen wrote to Mildred to assure her that he not forgotten them and explained that he was actively working on their case. Meanwhile, unbeknownst to Judge Bazile or the Caroline County sheriff's department, Mildred and Richard had returned to Virginia and were secretly staying in a nearby county. They still had their residence in the District of Columbia, in case they needed to flee Virginia at a moment's notice, but the pull to be near families and friends was stronger than their fear of being rearrested.

Judge Bazile was Cohen's remaining obstacle to getting the case before the Virginia courts again. For advice, the ACLU lawyer turned to Chester James Antieau, his old law professor at Georgetown University in Washington, DC. Antieau did more than teach law; he was active in civil rights legal challenges, which he hoped would bring about social change. When Cohen visited Antieau, he found that another of the professor's former students had also stopped by for a visit the same day, and the professor introduced the two. Philip J. Hirschkop had earned his law degree in 1964, a few years after Cohen, and immediately became immersed in civil rights litigation in the South. Shortly after finishing law school, Hirschkop had gone to Mississippi to fight for civil rights through the courts, and he was familiar with the tactics states often used to defend their Jim Crow laws. By the end of their visit, the two lawyers had joined forces. Hirschkop offered Cohen a potential way to bypass Judge Bazile or force him to respond. He suggested to Cohen that they file a class-action lawsuit with US District Court for the Eastern District of Virginia to request that a panel of three federal judges address the issue of Virginia's ban on mixed marriages.

In October 1964, the lawyers asked the federal court for "a preliminary injunction [order] against the Commonwealth of Virginia" to allow the Lovings to return together to the state and await a decision of the three-judge panel without fear of being taken into custody again. The lawyers also asked the federal court to "decide upon the constitutionality of" the statutes upon which the Lovings' arrests and convictions had been based. In their motion, the lawyers described these laws as "solely for the purpose of keeping the Negro people in the badges and bonds of slavery."

The Lovings' lawyers couldn't admit to the federal judges that the couple was defying Judge Bazile's order and already living in Virginia, because their motion for the injunction claimed the sentence had caused "irreparable injury." Nor did they wish to cause Richard and Mildred more difficulties with state authorities. Despite that, federal district Judge John D. Butzner Jr. saw no permanent injury and denied the lawyers' request for an injunction. At the same time, he allowed that a three-judge panel would address the constitutionality of the Lovings' arrests and of Virginia's ban on interracial marriage if the state failed to provide an opinion to Cohen's earlier motion to set aside the couple's sentences. Butzner gave the state ninety days to respond. If the state would not issue an opinion on the Lovings' sentences, the federal court would do so. Meanwhile, Hirschkop, Judge Butzner, and Virginia's assistant attorney general, Robert D. McIlwaine III, had worked out an informal agreement—a truce—that allowed the Lovings to start living in a county near Caroline County without fear of arrest. In the event that political pressure got too hot for the attorney general and he was forced to rearrest them, he promised to give them a week's notice so they could return to Washington.

The Lovings' lives returned to something resembling normal. Until the deal had been struck, Richard had been staying at his parents' house in Caroline County during the day, venturing out only at night to meet up with Mildred and the children, who stayed at her sister's house in a nearby Virginia county. Now they found a house of their own. Mildred had what she had longed for in Washington, DC—a place where their children could roam through fields and climb trees. They enrolled the children in a local school.

Judge Bazile waited until almost the end of the ninety-day period set down by the federal district judge before fixing a January 1965 date to hear Cohen's motion to vacate the charges against the Lovings. The outcome of the hearing was pretty much what Cohen and Hirschkop expected. The judge dismissed the notion that the couple's sentences were cruel and unusual "by citing cases from the 1820s." The judge reasoned that "each one of them can come to Caroline separately to visit his or her people as often as they please," just not with each other. As to Cohen's claim that their arrests and the racial integrity laws they were based upon violated the Fourteenth Amendment, the judge quoted several cases which held marriage "belongs to the exclusive control of the States." As Judge Bazile viewed it, the laws regulating marriage belonged to the states rather than to the federal government. A marriage that was legal in one state could be declared "unlawful and absolutely void" by another. Hirschkop noted, however, that "when Judge Bazile rendered his opinion, he couldn't have done us a bigger favor," by what he wrote next: "Almighty God created the races white, black, yellow, malay and red, and he placed them on separate continents. . . . The fact that he separated the races shows that he did not intend for the races to mix."

41

Judge Leon M. Bazile was born in 1890 and grew up in a segregated South that never questioned the wisdom of the Caucasian, or white, race that made the rules. Sixty-eight years of age when Richard and Mildred first came before his court, he never changed his opinion about their case or his ideas about mixed marriage. He died a few months before the US Supreme Court's 1967 ruling in *Loving v. Virginia*.

He continued then, cautioning Richard and Mildred that under Virginia law the "marriage between a white person and any colored person [is] a felony," and they would be known as felons the rest of their lives.

A few days after Judge Bazile's opinion came down, the Loving case was back before the federal district court. On January 27, 1965, while Cohen and Hirschkop tried to convince the panel of judges to take over jurisdiction, McIlwaine, representing Virginia, argued that the case should be heard by the justices of the state's supreme court. The federal judges offered their opinion on February 12, agreeing with the state's lawyer that the Lovings needed to turn first to the Supreme Court of Virginia before appealing to the federal system. Their decision wasn't a surprise to Cohen and Hirschkop because it is customary to require that cases exhaust appeals at the state level before the federal courts will step in. This gives the state courts an opportunity to reconsider the constitutional issues at play and reverse earlier decisions if need be. But in their ruling, the federal justices said the state court also had to address the constitutional issue of its statute against mixed-race marriages. The three-judge panel didn't stop there. In a victory of sorts for Richard and Mildred, the judges also ruled that during the appeal process the couple could live in Virginia legally. For the first time since 1959, the Lovings were allowed to visit their family and friends together, without fear of arrest.

Neither Cohen nor Hirschkop expected the outcome in the Supreme Court of Virginia to be any different than it had been in the circuit court before Judge Bazile. But it was a necessary step to get the case before the US Supreme Court. Feeling hopeful about their future, Mildred told reporters at the time, "All we want to do is go back to Virginia, build a home, and raise our children. We loved each other and got married. We are not marrying the state. The law should allow a person to marry anyone

43

he wants." Richard, who was unusually vocal during the interview, told reporters: "They said I had to leave the state once, and I left with my wife. If necessary, I will leave Virginia again with my wife, but I am not going to divorce her." For him, "leaving home was the hardest part of it."

The number of states with statutes against mixed marriages had fallen from twenty-four in 1958 to nineteen in 1963. Among those still holding to their Jim Crow marriage laws were the eleven Southern states that had formed the Confederacy. These states were joined by Maryland, West Virginia, Kentucky, Missouri, Oklahoma, Indiana, Wyoming, and Delaware, although Indiana and Wyoming repealed their laws in 1965. But more and more, the laws were coming under scrutiny. Only the month before, in December 1964, a case known as *McLaughlin v. Florida* went before the US Supreme Court. In the *McLaughlin* case, Dewey McLaughlin, a black man, and Connie Hoffman, a white woman, had been charged with interracial cohabitation, or living together. Marriage for the two had not been an option since mixed marriages were illegal in Florida. The state had no law against an unmarried white couple or unmarried black couple living together. McLaughlin and Hoffman believed they were being discriminated against and took their case to court. When it finally reached the US Supreme Court, the couple received a partial victory. The Supreme Court justices sidestepped Florida's law against racially mixed marriages, but it struck down the state's law that barred an unwed, mixed-race couple from living together as a violation of the equal protection clause of the Fourteenth Amendment. Many court observers saw *McLaughlin* as a first step to striking down the marriage statutes.

In Virginia, Cohen and Hirschkop went before the state supreme court and said that Judge Bazile had made a mistake when he held that Virginia's laws against mixed marriages were legal and not at odds with

As the case was on appeal, the Lovings were allowed to live in Virginia, at first by an informal agreement and later by order of a panel of three federal judges. Here, the family sits on the porch of their Central Point home in 1967 (back row, left to right: Peggy, Mildred, and Richard; front row, left to right: Donald and Sidney).

both "the Constitution of Virginia and the fourteenth amendment to the Federal Constitution." They claimed Bazile had gotten it wrong when he sentenced the couple. According to the lawyers, the judge had broken Virginia's own sentencing code, which called for "reasonable limits" to suspended sentences. Twenty-five years, they believed, was a long time for a court to exert its influence over anyone.

In mounting their case before the Virginia high court, the Lovings' lawyers turned to a 1948 California Supreme Court decision, which had led to California's laws against racially mixed marriages being overturned: "If the right to marry is a fundamental right, then it must be conceded that an infringement of that right by means of a racial restriction is an unlawful infringement of one's liberty." The California case, known as *Perez v. Sharp*, was the first time a state court had recognized that statutes which prohibited mixed-race marriages violated the equal protection clause of the Fourteenth Amendment. Nonetheless, Harry L. Carrico, a justice of the Supreme Court of Virginia, wrote that the laws against mixed marriages had been "fully investigated [by the US Supreme Court] and their constitutionality was upheld."

In truth, the US Supreme Court had never directly confronted the legalities or illegalities of laws that prohibited interracial marriages. Judge Carrico agreed with the Bazile ruling that the Lovings had violated a legal Virginia law, but he also ruled that the lower-court judge had incorrectly sentenced them. "The purpose," he stated, "which the trial court should reasonably have sought . . . was that the defendants not continue to violate" the state code, and that they "not again cohabit as man and wife in this state." In a unanimous decision by the Supreme Court of Virginia, he returned the case to Judge Bazile's court for resentencing. *Text continued on page 50*

The Supreme Court of the United States hears cases that involve constitutional law. People who want a narrow interpretation of the Constitution hold that courts should be bound by the exact words contained in the document, or the original intent of its framers (authors). Those who embrace the notion that the Constitution is a living document, one that changes with the times, think courts should understand and interpret it more broadly. They maintain that the needs of the nation should help to define the document.

As their case made its way through the courts, the Lovings were hopeful about its outcome, but Richard commented that if need be he would leave Virginia and return to Washington, DC, with his wife and three children. He was committed to the couple's love and to their marriage. Here they are seen in a playful moment.

Cohen and Hirschkop now prepared for the US Supreme Court, while Mildred and Richard returned to their lives in rural Virginia. Though they were able to remain there without fear of arrest, since their case still was under appeal, gone was the quiet, private life the couple wished for and had been accustomed to when they first married. The editors of *Life* magazine, sensing the case was an important one, sent photographer Grey Villet to record images of the family so the magazine's readers would have a better understanding of the couple behind the case. Hirschkop opposed the Lovings' involvement in the *Life* project, fearing the publicity would not benefit their case, but Cohen, who had political ambitions, was in favor of it. In the end, Cohen won the dispute, and Villet's photo-essay, scaled back from the original planned article, was published in March 1966 under the title "The Crime of Being Married." It pictured the Lovings at weekend drag races and doing mundane chores around the house, as well as showing the children climbing trees and playing in fields. At about the same time, filmmaker Hope Ryden began recording footage for a documentary on the Lovings. Again, Hirschkop had not favored the publicity, but Ryden agreed not to release anything until after the case had been decided. The film Ryden envisioned never came to be because she tucked the footage in a closet and essentially forgot about it.

Meanwhile, Cohen and Hirschkop strategized to get the case to the US Supreme Court. They had to show that the Virginia courts, by enforcing the state's laws, had violated the US Constitution before the court would agree to hear their arguments. They raised several constitutional questions, primarily: Were Virginia's statutes that banned interracial marriage a violation of the due process and equal protection clauses of the Fourteenth Amendment to the US Constitution? Were these statutes a violation of the constitutional right to privacy and right to marry? In July, Cohen and Hirschkop requested the Supreme Court hear their appeal.

Mildred and Richard were aware that the case, if the Supreme Court justices agreed to hear it, could have an impact on the lives of other mixed-race couples. "We have thought about other people," Richard had explained in the March 1966 *Life* article, "but we are not doing it just because somebody had to do it and we wanted to be the ones. We are doing it for *us*—because we want to live here [in Virginia]."

On December 12, 1966, the Lovings won their day in court when the US Supreme Court agreed to hear their case. Now Cohen and Hirschkop were faced with writing a legal argument that would convince the Supreme Court justices to strike down Virginia's ban on interracial marriage. For the two young lawyers, neither of whom had ever stood before the high court to make a case, it was a daunting challenge.

Cohen and Hirschkop both realized they had to get the facts right before appearing in front of the justices of the US Supreme Court. The Civil Rights Act of 1964 was already law, as was the Voting Rights Act of 1965, which aimed to abolish barriers at the state and local levels that prevented blacks from casting ballots in elections. The Lovings' lawyers both believed that marriage statutes that infringed on an individual's right to choose a mate were the last barrier to equality and social justice in the United States, and that these codes' real purpose was to raise up one group of people socially and economically and keep another group down. "This is strictly a segregation problem," maintained Hirschkop. He believed the Southern states, those that had made up the Confederacy, saw the federal government as an oppressor, denying them their constitutional rights. In his own words, he held that the states "don't want to argue the segregation. . . . They never want to argue the individual right of the person. They always want to argue the right of the state."

As for Richard and Mildred, they continued with their simple lives in rural Virginia. Occasionally, they would have a night out in Bowling Green,

The Lovings' lawyers, Bernard S. Cohen (center) and Philip J. Hirschkop (right), and an unidentified man hold a press conference in January 1967.

but generally they kept to themselves, their families, and a small circle of friends. They didn't have a telephone, so their lawyers had to leave messages with a relative if they wished to communicate with them. But for the most part, the lawyers didn't involve the Lovings in their legal plan as it unfolded. Beyond the initial meeting with Cohen, for which no notes exist, Hirschkop estimates they met with the couple fewer than half a dozen times. But he was impressed with how Richard stuck by his wife and their children. As a white man, Hirschkop pointed out, he could have left Mildred with no consequences to himself, but he chose to honor the love they shared. *Text continued on page 58*

African Americans, one with *VOTE* on his forehead, march from Selma toward Montgomery, Alabama, in 1965 to encourage Congress to pass a voting rights act to guarantee them a voice in the political system.

Richard owned a race car with two African American friends and often spent his free time adjusting the car's engine. Attending local drag races, which Richard's team often won, was a typical weekend pastime for the couple before, during, and after their case made it to the US Supreme Court.

As the attorneys prepared their line of reasoning for the US Supreme Court and sought advice from other ACLU lawyers and anyone else willing to offer it, groups with an interest in the case's outcome weighed in with information to help the court's justices reach a decision. The National Association for the Advancement of Colored People (NAACP), a group that had gained a reputation for fighting for equal rights through the courts, tackled a position that Virginia had used in 1955 and which it feared the state would attempt to use again. In a Virginia Supreme Court case known as *Naim v. Naim*, Han Say Naim, a Chinese sailor, and Ruby Elaine Naim, a white Virginia woman, had been legally married in North Carolina. But when Ruby filed for an annulment from Han in Virginia a year after their marriage, Han protested and took his quarrel all the way to the state supreme court. The state's high court, however, ruled that on the basis of the Racial Integrity Act of 1924, the Naim marriage was not legal in Virginia and, in fact, didn't exist at all. What was legal in North Carolina, the court held, had no relevance in Virginia. Han then appealed the Virginia ruling to the US Supreme Court, but the appeal was turned down.

Naim is important because in subsequent cases, including the Loving appeals before both Judge Bazile and Justice Carrico, it had been pointed to as evidence that the Supreme Court had upheld interracial marriage bans. The Supreme Court had done no such thing. The high court had chosen not to hear the case because some of the justices were fearful of creating a public backlash so soon after the 1954 decision in *Brown v. Board of Education*. The NAACP thought it was time for the high court to take an unmistakable stand on mixed-race marriages and wrote a brief both to support the Loving case and to discredit the faulty reasoning applied to *Naim*.

The National Catholic Conference for Interracial Justice (NCCIJ), which represented Catholic bishops, was another group that filed a brief as friend of the court. Cohen and Hirschkop planned to say that Virginia was in violation of the Fourteenth Amendment, but the NCCIJ took a First Amendment stand. This amendment guarantees that people can choose whom they associate with, without fear of government interference. They urged other religious groups to join them in writing to the court, saying the prohibition of mixed-race marriages was immoral, unchristian, and unconstitutional.

Only North Carolina supported Virginia's claim that marriage was set aside for states to regulate, not the federal government. North Carolina's attorney general, T. W. Bruton, prepared a brief in which he claimed that the Fourteenth Amendment should have no bearing on the case. In it, Bruton could not control his distaste for interracial marriages or his anger at the Supreme Court for interfering in what he insisted were states' rights.

With more experience in civil rights law than Cohen, most of the case preparation fell to Hirschkop. But Hirschkop also recognized his limitations as a new lawyer. He and Cohen traveled to New York to seek the advice of other ACLU attorneys there. Their former Georgetown University law professor, Chester Antieau, reviewed and refined what Hirschkop had written. They also turned to William D. Zabel, a human rights lawyer, and Arthur L. Berney, a constitutional law professor at Boston College in Massachusetts, both of whom also reviewed the brief and urged Hirschkop and Cohen to seek a wide-reaching decision from the justices—one that would strike down all racial marriage laws, not just those in Virginia. Finally, Hirschkop turned to William Kunstler, a well-known lawyer he'd first met while working in Mississippi, for advice on how best to approach the nine justices sitting on the Supreme Court bench, especially those who were known conservatives.

On April 10, 1967, Cohen and Hirschkop climbed the steps to the US Supreme Court to make their oral arguments before Chief Justice Earl Warren and the other eight justices. Robert D. McIlwaine III, the assistant attorney general of Virginia, would defend the state's laws and customs. Before the hearing, Hirschkop had written to the Lovings to invite them to attend, but Mildred phoned to say that she was nervous about the outcome and would rather remain in Virginia, unless she could be of help to the two attorneys. As Cohen tells it, he also spoke to Mildred and Richard to invite them to attend the hearing, but Richard said, "I probably wouldn't understand," so they didn't even go.

When the court was called to order in the case of *Richard Perry Loving, et al. v. Virginia*, Hirschkop planned to speak to the equal protection portion of the Fourteenth Amendment. He would seek to show how the Jim Crow marriage laws were handed down from the days of enslavement and were meant to keep one group of people as second-class citizens. Hirschkop followed Zabel's advice and would also show that the Virginia statutes were unjust: They didn't allow for two mature, consenting adults of different racial backgrounds to marry, which denied them equal rights. Cohen would tackle due process, or fairness. He would put forward that a couple who was legally married in one state ought to have the right to move to any other state without fear of arrest or loss of the benefits that marriage grants.

Hirschkop began with a traditional greeting to the court: "Mr. Chief Justice, Associate Justices; may it please the Court." He then went on to tell the court that he and Cohen hoped to show that Virginia's interracial marriage prohibition laws did not stem from the welfare of the state or concern for the children of mixed marriages, but from slavery laws in the 1600s, which had prohibited marriages between whites and the enslaved. These laws had been changed over time to narrowly define what a white person was in order to keep one race superior to others in social and economic position. Speaking to Virginia's Racial Integrity Act, Hirschkop pointed out that it did nothing to protect "the racial integrity of the Negro race, only . . . the white race." He added that the mid-1920s were historically important because it was during this time that states with these rules began to require citizens to register their race before a marriage license would be issued.

In responding to a question Chief Justice Earl Warren had asked, Hirschkop explained that at one time almost all states had laws that prohibited mixed-race marriages, but now there were only sixteen that had these regulations.

Hirschkop asked the justices to consider only one thing: "May a state proscribe [forbid] a marriage between two adult consenting individuals because of their race?"

Before he concluded, Hirschkop brought up Judge Bazile's remark about "Almighty God" and the races. "It's a fundamentally ludicrous quote," he said. The laws banning mixed marriages, he continued, were meant "to keep the slaves in their place, were prolonged to keep the slaves in their place, and in truth the Virginia laws still view the Negro race as a slave race." Urging the court to come to the right ruling, he insisted that these statutes "rob the Negro race of its dignity, and only a decision which will reach the full body of these laws of the state of Virginia will change that."

Cohen rose to address the court, but he knew that Virginia's assistant attorney general would hold that the Fourteenth Amendment had no bearing, that the amendment's authors never intended to include issues of marriage. The state's attorney had done so when he stood before the three-judge panel in federal district court and again when *Text continued on page 64*

At the Supreme Court, Bernard S. Cohen, one of the attorneys in the case, argued that the Virginia laws did not protect the children of mixed-race marriages. These children might be denied inheritance rights because of the state's view that the marriages were invalid and illegal. Peggy, Donald, and Sidney (left to right) are caught at play in the fields near their Virginia home.

the case went before the Supreme Court of Virginia. Cohen's strategy was to stop that line of thinking even before McIlwaine could make it. Cohen contended that if the framers of the amendment had meant to exclude these statutes, "it would have taken but a single phrase" for them to say it didn't apply to issues of marriage. Instead, he maintained that the language of the amendment was purposely vague and "meant to include equal protection for Negroes. That was at the very heart of it."

Cohen turned to the Lovings and their children and spoke about how marriage laws based on race or skin color put the couple at a disadvantage. Richard and Mildred have a right, he said, "to wake up in the morning, or to go to sleep at night, knowing that the sheriff will not be knocking on their door or shining a light in their face in the privacy of their bedroom, for 'illicit cohabitation.'" He pointed out that the couple had the right to know "that should they not awake in the morning their children would have the right to inherit from them. . . . They have the right to be secure in knowing that if they go to sleep and do not wake in the morning, that one of them, a survivor of them, has the right to Social Security benefits. All of these are denied to them" under the laws that prohibit marriage between a white person and a black person.

Cohen recalled the telephone conversation with Richard and Mildred in which he had invited them to attend the Supreme Court proceedings. Richard's comment neatly summarized what the entire case was about. "No one can articulate it better," said the lawyer, "than Richard Loving, when he said to me: 'Mr. Cohen, tell the Court I love my wife, and it is just unfair that I can't live with her in Virginia.'" This, to Cohen, said everything that needed to be said about the inequality of the interracial marriage statutes.

Justice Hugo L. Black asked if Cohen and Hirschkop were suggesting that the court strike down all of the racially based marriage laws.

"Your Honor," Cohen responded, "we should be very pleased to have a decision from this Court that all of the statutes are unconstitutional."

The Lovings' lawyer suggested the court should ask McIlwaine what danger a mixed-race marriage poses to the state or to the people of the state. He charged, "This question has been carefully avoided."

It came as no surprise that McIlwaine disagreed with Hirschkop's and Cohen's claims. He suggested that there were only two sections of the Virginia code that the justices should consider. "These statutes in their combined effect, prohibit white people from marrying colored people and colored people from marrying white people . . . and forbids citizens of Virginia of either race from leaving the State with intent and purpose of evading this law." The assistant attorney general hoped to hold the court to a decision that affected only these two sections of state law. If he was successful, and only these sections were declared unequal in their application, Virginia legislators could then revise the laws to say that whites could marry only whites, blacks only blacks, Asians only Asians, and so on, until they had accounted for every group residing in the state. Hirschkop and Cohen, on the other hand, had tried, through their arguments, to steer the justices toward a broader ruling that would end race-based marriage laws.

Hirschkop and Cohen had maintained that the state violated the Fourteenth Amendment. McIlwaine's position was that the amendment did not apply to the case before the court. He felt that "this Court under the Fourteenth Amendment is not authorized to infringe the power of the State." He also claimed that it was a legitimate right of Virginia or any other state to pass legislation to prevent "sociological, psychological evils which attend interracial marriages."

McIlwaine went on to say that the US Supreme Court had held over the years "that society is structured on the institution of marriage" and "that it has more to do with a welfare and civilizations of a people that any other institutions [sic]." It was the function of the state to make sure that marriages were successful. To support his argument, he quoted from a book by Dr. Albert I. Gordon, a rabbi, sociologist, and anthropologist. McIlwaine claimed it was the most "definitive book on intermarriage." Gordon's views supported those of Virginia, specifically that the state had a right and a necessity to prohibit marriage between whites and blacks for the well-being of the population and society. But Gordon's book also was the only so-called expert source McIlwaine used to support his case. The chief justice asked if the same might be said of marriages that crossed religious lines. McIlwaine claimed that religious pressures weren't as great as racial pressures, and continued to say that according to Gordon the children of mixed marriages have more psychological problems than do children of single-race marriages. This was because, he said, people who entered into mixed-race marriages "have a rebellious attitude toward society, self-hatred, neurotic tendencies, immaturity, and other detrimental . . . factors."

Justice Potter Stewart interrupted McIlwaine, saying, "You don't know what is cause and what is effect. . . . I suppose [it] could be argued . . . that marriages of this kind are sometimes unsuccessful [because of] the existence of the kind of laws that are in issue here."

Chief Justice Earl Warren challenged McIlwaine by asking the assistant attorney general if his argument wasn't the same one heard in *Brown v. Board of Education*, that "whites would be injured by having to go to school with the—with the Negroes?"

Before the oral arguments concluded, Bernard Cohen rose once again to ask the justices not to limit their decision to the statutes that McIlwaine said were the only issues before the court. He reminded them that if they did, then under Virginia laws Richard and Mildred could be arrested again when Virginia rewrote its laws. Because their marriage was considered void, or invalid, in that state, their children would not have the same rights of inheritance as children of single-race parents. Mildred or Richard, as a survivor of the other, would not be entitled to the same benefits that single-race couples had. He urged the court to be bold in its decision and to bring constitutional justice to those who had been denied it. He asked the men sitting behind the raised bench in their black robes "to invalidate the entire statutory scheme."

A little over two months later, on June 12, 1967, the US Supreme Court announced its unanimous decision. It ruled that states could not outlaw marriages between whites and nonwhites. The ruling was bold, as Cohen had urged, and it was disapproving enough to leave no doubt that the racial marriage laws remaining in fifteen states were relics of the past as well.

Chief Justice Earl Warren delivered the court's opinion. "We conclude," he wrote, "that these statutes cannot stand consistently with the Fourteenth Amendment." They appeared to the court to be an endorsement of white supremacy. In reviewing the state's arguments, Warren agreed "that marriage is a social relation subject to the State's police power," but he also said that its power to regulate marriage isn't unlimited. "Marriage is one of the 'basic civil rights of man,' fundamental to our very existence and survival," the opinion continued. "The Freedom to marry, or not marry, a person of another race resides with the individual and cannot be infringed by the State." The court ruled that the convictions of Richard Perry Loving and Mildred Jeter Loving must be reversed.

67

John F. Davis, the clerk to the Supreme Court, notified Bernard S. Cohen by telegram on June 12, 1967, that the Supreme Court had reached a decision in *Loving v. Virginia* and that he had mailed the opinion.

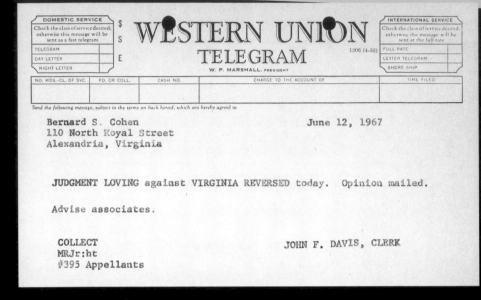

WESTERN UNION
TELEGRAM
W. P. MARSHALL, PRESIDENT

DOMESTIC SERVICE
Check the class of service desired; otherwise this message will be sent as a fast telegram

TELEGRAM
DAY LETTER
NIGHT LETTER

INTERNATIONAL SERVICE
Check the class of service desired; otherwise the message will be sent at the full rate

FULL RATE
LETTER TELEGRAM
SHORE SHIP

NO. WDS.-CL. OF SVC. | PD. OR COLL. | CASH NO. | CHARGE TO THE ACCOUNT OF | TIME FILED

Send the following message, subject to the terms on back hereof, which are hereby agreed to

Bernard S. Cohen   June 12, 1967
110 North Royal Street
Alexandria, Virginia

JUDGMENT LOVING against VIRGINIA REVERSED today. Opinion mailed.

Advise associates.

COLLECT   JOHN F. DAVIS, CLERK
MRJr:ht
#395 Appellants

Nine years after Sheriff Garnett Brooks burst into the couple's bedroom and arrested them, Mildred and Richard found their way home to Caroline County. Richard built a home for his bride on the land his father had given them as a wedding present, and the couple lived happily among their family and friends for the next eight years. In late June 1975, Richard and Mildred were returning home from an evening out in Bowling Green, when a drunk driver failed to heed a stop sign and slammed into their vehicle. Richard was killed instantly. Mildred never remarried and continued to live in the house Richard had built for her, surrounded by her family, until her death in May 2008.

Neither Richard nor Mildred had been political during their lives. They did what they did out of personal need—a need to be among friends, to be with their families, and to raise their own family in a familiar place they wanted to call home. But what is personal often is political. Accidental civil rights activists who never sought the public spotlight, this quiet couple, with the help of their lawyers, laid out a path that another generation of people seeking marriage equality would follow.

5 — AFTER *LOVING*

Even before the Stonewall riots of 1969, when members of the gay, or homosexual, community resisted police during an early morning raid at the Stonewall Inn in New York City's Greenwich Village neighborhood, gay people had been seeking equality with their hetero-sexual brothers and sisters. They had only a dim hope of ever achieving it.

Despite the Emma Lazarus poem inscribed at the base of the Statue of Liberty, which reads, "Give me your tired, your poor, / Your huddled masses yearning to breathe free," gay individuals, or those perceived to be, simply were not welcome in the United States, and certainly not as the equals of heterosexuals. Laws discriminated against them; indeed, they made their relationships criminal. They offered them no legal protections if they were fired from jobs or if landlords refused to rent to them because of their sexual orientation or gender identity. They were often the victims of physical violence by hoodlums and by police departments, who sometimes blackmailed gay individuals who wanted to keep this part of their lives private.

But when police raided the Stonewall Inn on the morning of June 28, the gay community had had enough. People were tired of being victimized, of being held to second-class status, and they spontaneously decided to fight back in a series of violent demonstrations. That morning marked the beginning of the modern gay fight for civil rights and equality under the law in the US.

The Stonewall riots were a turning point, but even before 1969 gay individuals were challenging the way things were. In Minnesota, a law student named Richard John "Jack" Baker and a librarian, James Michael McConnell, decided on March 10, 1967, Jack's twenty-fifth birthday, to marry. Within the gay community, marriage had never been a realistic, legal option. Most gay men and women lived in secrecy, fearful of the criticism and disapproval their sexuality might bring. But when Richard and Mildred set out on their legal journey for the right to build a home together in Virginia and to celebrate their love, it changed things. For the two men, Jack and Michael, their decision was about personal liberty and the freedom to marry in order to form a bond that the state would recognize.

In May 1970, they applied for a marriage license and were denied by the clerk of the Fourth Judicial District Court in Hennepin County. They filed a lawsuit against the clerk, and the case eventually reached the Minnesota Supreme Court, where their attorney drew on *Loving* to argue that the laws were attempting to make heterosexuals a superior group to homosexuals, much like Cohen and Hirschkop held that Virginia's laws were meant to support white supremacy.

In October 1971, Minnesota's Supreme Court handed down its ruling, which rejected the idea that *Loving* had anything to do with their case. When their lawsuit advanced, the US Supreme Court declined to give it a hearing because it didn't view the matter as an issue of constitutional law.

James Michael McConnell (left) and Richard John "Jack" Baker applying for a Minnesota marriage license. Although they were denied at first, Baker, a law student, found nothing in the state code that prevented two men from marrying. They applied again in another county after Baker changed his name to something either a male or female might use—Pat Lyn. They were granted a license in 1971.

By then, Baker had found a way to outfox the law—a sleight of hand, if you will. To give them inheritance and other legal rights, McConnell legally adopted Baker. Then because of Minnesota's gender-neutral marriage laws, Baker changed his name to Pat Lyn, which might have been appropriate for either a male or a female. They applied again for a marriage license, this time in another county, and received one from Blue Earth County's unsuspecting clerk of the Fifth Judicial District Court. They were married in Minneapolis on September 3, 1971.

McConnell and Baker were married on September 3, 1971. Since same-sex marriages were unheard of at the time and finding a cake topper featuring a male-male couple was impossible, a friend came to the rescue by purchasing two traditional ornaments, cutting them apart, and gluing the two men in top hats together.

Although they became the first male couple to legally wed, their marriage was not recorded by the clerk but neither had it been revoked. It also was not recognized by the federal government. Even so, their action helped to ignite a spark that had been lingering in the hearts of many gay men and women since the *Loving* decision.

73

Over the next couple of decades, the gay community kept whittling away at laws that made its members second-class citizens. Time and again these cases turned to the *Loving* opinion to make their arguments. In 1982, Michael Hardwick was arrested in Atlanta, Georgia, when a police officer witnessed Hardwick, in the privacy of the man's own bedroom, having physical relations with another man. The case, known as *Bowers v. Hardwick*, worked its way to the US Supreme Court, where in a five-to-four decision, Hardwick lost. Nonetheless, the case focused attention on the inequality of the law—what was criminal for Hardwick to do was not illegal for a heterosexual couple. It also brought attention to the invasive nature of some laws and questioned if states have a right to invade the privacy of a person's bedroom.

By the 1990s, the gay community began to look at state constitutions, rather than at the Fourteenth Amendment used in *Loving*. Many state constitutions were far more comprehensive than the US Constitution in extending equality and fairness to all. In a same-sex marriage case that came before the Hawaii Supreme Court, it was acknowledged that marriage was a fundamental right of two people, but the question was whether to extend those benefits to couples of the same gender. The state needed to prove an overwhelming reason why marriage should be restricted. When the ruling came down in December 1996, the court said the state had failed to make its case. The state had found no compelling reason, no valid basis to ban same-sex marriage.

The Hawaii ruling set off legislative alarm bells. Both in the state and beyond its borders, legislators began to tighten the language of their constitutions. These amendments restricted marriage to one man and one woman, or to opposite-sex couples. To calm gay activists, they offered same-sex couples domestic partnerships and civil unions instead, which granted some of the benefits that came with marriage, but not all, not equality. Many religious groups became horrified that an institution they viewed as sacred, holy, and inviolable, despite the divorce rate, would be extended to same-sex couples. Conservative individuals joined them. Before long, these opponents began to push for the US Constitution to be amended to define marriage. But the federal constitution was designed to be difficult to change, so in the end Congress put forward the Defense of Marriage Act (DOMA), which President Bill Clinton signed in October 1996. DOMA prevented domestic partners and other same-sex couples from collecting federal benefits or filing joint tax returns, among other things. This act of Congress created a separate and unequal status for same-sex couples.

As a new century dawned, the fight for same-sex marriage continued. The Netherlands became the first country to legalize same-sex marriage in 2001. Other countries soon followed its lead. In November 2003, the Massachusetts Supreme Judicial Court ruled that the state could not legally ban same-sex marriages. Chief Justice Margaret H. Marshall wrote, "The Massachusetts Constitution affirms the dignity and equality of all individuals. It forbids the creation of second-class citizens." Connecting the court's ruling to *Loving v. Virginia*, the justice continued, "Recognizing the right of an individual to marry a person of the same sex will not diminish the validity or dignity of opposite-sex marriage, any more than recognizing the right of an individual to marry a person of a different race devalues the marriage of a person who marries someone of her own race." The state began issuing marriage licenses to same-sex couples in May 2004.

Other states soon followed Massachusetts, but DOMA and a threat of a federal constitutional amendment still lingered, casting a shadow over the whole question of marriage, since federal statutes overrule state laws. But DOMA faced a reckoning in the case of Edith Windsor. In 2009, the Internal Revenue Service sent Windsor a huge tax bill upon the death of her wife, Thea Spyer. Windsor and Spyer had been legally married in Canada in 2007 and lived in New York, which by law recognized their marriage. When they'd registered as domestic partners in 1993, the couple had already been together thirty years.

When Spyer died, she left her estate to Windsor, but because their marriage was not recognized by federal law, the Internal Revenue Service sent Windsor a bill for $363,000, which it said was owed in taxes on the estate. DOMA defined marriage as a union between one man and one woman. Had Windsor's marriage to Spyer been legal in the eyes of the federal government, Windsor would have qualified as a spouse and no tax bill would have been levied. On November 9, 2010, she filed a lawsuit seeking to have DOMA declared unconstitutional. In its ruling, the court agreed with Windsor and ordered the government to refund the money. When the government appealed the case to the US Supreme Court, a majority of the justices agreed with the lower court. In *United States v. Windsor*, the court ruled in a five-to-four decision on June 26, 2013, that the purpose of DOMA was to put same-sex couples at a disadvantage and a violation of the Fifth Amendment's guarantee of equal protection.

By 2015, thirty-six states and the District of Columbia had legalized same-sex marriage either by law, by court rulings, or by vote. Ohio was one of the holdout states which still banned same-sex marriage, so when James Obergefell and John Arthur wanted legal recognition of their relationship, they went to Maryland to marry. Arthur, however, was terminally ill, and both men wanted Obergefell listed as surviving spouse on his death certificate when the time came. While the local registrar of vital statistics agreed that discriminating against the couple was unconstitutional, Ohio Governor John Kasich vowed to fight it in court and ordered the Ohio attorney general's office to defend the state's same-sex marriage ban. Obergefell filed a lawsuit against Kasich. As the case made its way through the courts, it was combined with similar lawsuits from Michigan, Ohio, Kentucky, and Tennessee, until it eventually went to the US Supreme Court as *Obergefell v. Hodges, Director, Ohio Department of Health* where the court was asked to resolve two questions. The first, does the due process clause of the Fourteenth Amendment apply to same-sex marriage and require states to issue a license to two people who are the same gender? And second, does the equal protection clause of the Fourteenth Amendment require states to recognize a same-sex marriage that was legally performed in another state?

In a landmark decision on June 26, 2015, the US Supreme Court reached back to *Loving v. Virginia* and other cases to render its decision. It agreed that bans against same-sex marriage were unconstitutional. In the majority opinion, Justice Anthony Kennedy wrote, "The right to marry is a fundamental right inherent in the liberty of the person, and under the Due Process and Equal Protection Clauses of the Fourteenth Amendment couples of the same-sex may not be deprived of that right and that liberty." Sadly, Arthur died before the case was resolved. In responding to the states' accusations that same-sex marriage demeaned opposite-sex marriage, Kennedy held that "far from seeking to devalue marriage, the petitioners seek it for themselves because of their respect—and need—for its privileges and responsibilities." *Text continued on page 80*

Dr. Thea Spyer and Edith Windsor (right) had been together for forty years when they legally married in Canada in 2007. When Spyer died in 2009, Windsor was hit with a tax bill of $363,000 because the federal government didn't recognize their marriage. In the midst of her grief, Windsor took the United States to court, and the Supreme Court ruled in her favor.

James Obergefell (seen here) and John Arthur went to Maryland to be legally married, but in their home state of Ohio, their marriage wasn't recognized as legal. It was a situation similar to the one Richard and Mildred Loving faced, where their legal Washington, DC, marriage was held to be void, or invalid, by Virginia authorities. When Arthur died, Obergefell sued Ohio to be recognized as Arthur's surviving spouse. The case eventually ended at the Supreme Court, which was charged with deciding whether marriages legally performed in one state should be recognized in states where those marriages were considered illegal.

Mildred Loving probably would have approved of the court's ruling. Years earlier, on June 12, 2007, she released a written statement in celebration of the fortieth anniversary of the *Loving* decision. In it she said, "I believe all Americans, no matter their race, no matter their sex, no matter their sexual orientation, should have that same freedom to marry." Doubtless, she never thought that the hopefulness contained in her letters to Bobby Kennedy and the ACLU would likewise lend hope to those seeking to overturn not a racial restriction, but one of gender, or that the case resulting from her desire to return home would cast a glimmer of light to the farthest corners of the country. The US Supreme Court understood that hope and that need. It ruled, "No union is more profound than marriage, for it embodies the highest ideals of love, fidelity, devotion, sacrifice, and family. In forming a marital union, two people become something greater than once they were. . . . They ask for equal dignity in the eyes of the law. The Constitution grants them that right."

AUTHOR'S NOTE

The South's stand against racially mixed marriages wasn't anything new. Statutes against such unions had existed since colonial times as a way to draw a line between the wealthy and powerful, and those who had been enslaved. Such racial barriers helped to keep the shameful system of discrimination in place.

The statutes that banned interracial marriage in the United States were known as "antimiscegenation" laws. Oddly, the word *miscegenation* wasn't even known until America's Civil War, when two Southern Democrats pretending to be Republicans coined it. David Goodman Croly and George Wakeman anonymously wrote a little booklet called *Miscegenation: The Theory of the Blending of the Races, Applied to the American White Man and Negro*. According to the booklet, the word stems "from the Latin *Miscere*, to mix, and *Genus*, race." It was meant to outrage Southern Democrats by suggesting the superiority of mixed races. It claimed that "when the President [Lincoln] proclaimed Emancipation he proclaimed also the mingling of the races. The one follows the other as surely as noonday follows sunrise." Hoping to elicit fear and indignation, the authors wrote, "The Republican party . . . demands that every black man in the land shall be free . . . that the plantations of the South shall be transferred to him from his rebel master . . ." In a South that celebrated its way of life and whose wealth had been built from the labor of enslaved black people, the duo's work must have been shocking, especially when they wrote, "The dark races must absorb the white." In other words, the races would intermarry.

Although the Confederacy lost the Civil War, the South refused to see its black citizens as social equals. It would have nothing to do with racial blending, despite the fact that in the past, white male slave-owners had sometimes impregnated enslaved females as a way to increase their wealth. The South had been a culture that measured prosperity in terms of the number of slaves one owned, and the children resulting from those owner-slave relationships were born enslaved. Marriage was another matter, however. Legislators had various explanations for making mixed-race marriages illegal. Generally, white lawmakers claimed they were protecting white citizens, especially white women, from an increasing number of nonwhite people. Others claimed that mixed marriages were immoral. They said that antimiscegenation laws were necessary for the common good of society and to protect public health, maintaining that children born to mixed marriages were mentally and physically inferior to those whose bloodlines ran pure. Oddly (or not so oddly given that white men wrote these laws), white women who crossed the color line and had children were punished more harshly than white men.

States routinely revised their laws to tighten racial definitions, but their intent was the same: to dictate whom a person could marry. In 1924, the state of Virginia passed and amended several restrictive statutes under the Preservation of Racial Integrity Act, which required proof of race in order to receive a marriage license. To assure that the Caucasian race remained pure, the act made it "unlawful for any white person in this State to marry any save a white person." It made an exception for those Virginians who claimed they were descended from Pocahontas, an indigenous Virginian (Indian), who married John Rolfe, a Jamestown colonist, although the legislature eventually did away with this special circumstance. The act was amended further to define a person of color as anyone with any

Negro blood whatsoever—the so-called "one drop rule," which was meant to protect whiteness, but which did nothing to preserve the integrity of the bloodlines of any other race. The Preservation of Racial Integrity Act remained in effect until the Supreme Court ruled in *Loving v. Virginia*.

With the Supreme Court ruling in *Loving v. Virginia* in 1967, those remaining states with antimiscegenation laws on the books reversed them. One holdout was Alabama, which did not officially make interracial marriage legal until November 2000, following a ballot referendum.

Sadly, only one of the Lovings' children, Peggy Fortune, is alive today. She still lives in Virginia and is the mother of three. Donald Loving, the couple's second son, died in 2000 at the age of forty-one. No details are available about the cause of his death. Sidney Jeter, the couple's oldest son, died on May 5, 2010. He was the father of six children, two of whom preceded him in death. Although Richard was the biological father of only Donald and Peggy, he acknowledged all three children as his own.

Mildred's grandson, Mark Loving, maintains that his grandmother was not black. "I know during those times, there were only two colors: white and blacks," he told NBC-12, the Richmond, Virginia, television station. "But she was Native American, both of her parents were Native American." As evidence, he points to their application for a marriage license, which classifies Mildred as Indian. However, only Richard's signature appears on the application, affirming that the information is "true, to the best of my knowledge and belief." In recorded interviews, Mildred referred to herself as colored and in her letter to the ACLU, she identified as "part negro, & part indian." Also, members of her family dispute that Mildred wrote the words attributed to her in the statement that was released on June 12, 2007, to celebrate the fortieth anniversary of the *Loving* decision.

Forty-seven years after Jack Baker (right) and Michael McConnell were married in Minneapolis, Minnesota, their marriage was declared legal and valid, making them the first same-sex couple to have legally married in the United States.

Bernard Cohen, born in Brooklyn, New York, continued his fight for civil rights by pursuing a career in politics after his success in *Loving v. Virginia*. He was elected to the Virginia House of Delegates in 1980 and served until 1996. Retired now, he continues to live in Virginia.

Philip Hirschkop, whom I interviewed for this book, still works as a civil rights lawyer in Virginia. He has defended Vietnam War protesters, fought for women's rights, and argued for teachers' rights. I am most grateful to him for taking the time to discuss the Loving case with me and for sharing a copy of Mildred's letter to the ACLU. Amazingly, he answered his own telephone!

Richard John "Jack" Baker's and Michael McConnell's 1971 marriage was officially recognized by the state of Minnesota in September 2018 in a district court ruling which said, "The marriage is declared to be in all respects valid." The federal government's Social Security Administration echoed this in a letter it sent to the couple on February 16, 2019, officially recognizing that their 1971 marriage was legal and that they both were entitled to each other's spousal benefits. In their seventies now, they continue to live in Minneapolis and were consulted for this book. Theirs was indeed the first same-sex marriage to be legally performed in the United States.

BIBLIOGRAPHY

(Sources consulted by the author.)

Books

Alko, Selina, and Sean Qualls. *The Case for Loving: The Fight for Interracial Marriage*. New York: Arthur A. Levine Books, 2015.*

Alonso, Karen. *Loving v. Virginia: Interracial Marriage* (Landmark Supreme Court Cases series). Berkeley Heights, NJ: Enslow Publishers, Inc., 2000.*

Botham, Fay. *Almighty God Created the Races: Christianity, Interracial Marriage, & American Law*. Chapel Hill, NC: The University of North Carolina Press, 2009.

Croly, David G. *Miscegenation: The Theory of the Blending of the Races, Applied to the American White Man and Negro*. London: Forgotten Books (FB&c Ltd.), 2018.

Curry, George E., editor. *The Best of Emerge Magazine*. New York: Ballantine Books, 2003.

Irons, Peter, and Stephanie Guitton. *May It Please the Court . . .: Transcripts of 23 Live Recordings of Landmark Cases as Argued before the Supreme Court*. New York: The New Press, 1993. (Primary Source)

Newbeck, Phyl. *Virginia Hasn't Always Been for Lovers: Interracial Marriage Bans and the Case of Richard and Mildred Loving*. Carbondale, IL: Southern Illinois University Press, 2004.

Paul, Darel E. *From Tolerance to Equality: How Elites Brought America to Same-Sex Marriage*. Waco, TX: Baylor University Press, 2018.

Porterfield, Jason. *Marriage Equality: Obergefell v. Hodges* (US Supreme Court Landmark Cases series). New York: Enslow Publishing, 2017.*

Powell, Patricia Hruby; Shadra Strickland, illustrator. *Loving vs. Virginia: A Documentary Novel of the Landmark Civil Rights Case*. San Francisco: Chronicle Books, 2017.*

Wallenstein, Peter. *Race, Sex, and the Freedom to Marry: Loving v. Virginia*. Lawrence, KS: University Press of Kansas, 2014.

Wallenstein, Peter. *Tell the Court I Love My Wife: Race, Marriage, and Law—An American History*. New York: St. Martin's Griffin, 2002.

Indicates a book specifically for young readers.

Film/Video

Loving. A Raindog Films and Big Beach Films production; written and directed by Jeff Nichols; 2016. Feature Film.

Loving Story, The. An Augusta Films production; directed by Nancy Buirski; written by Nancy Buirski and Susie Ruth Powell for HBO Documentary Films; 2011. DVD. (Primary Source)

Mr. & Mrs. Loving. Daniel L. Paulson Productions, in association with Hallmark Entertainment and Showtime Networks; directed and written by Richard Friedenberg; 1996. DVD television movie.

Magazines

"Crime of Being Married, The," *Life* magazine, March 18, 1966, pp. 85–91.

Star, Jack. "The Homosexual Couple," *Look* magazine, January 26, 1971, p. 69.

Valentine, Victoria. "When Love Was a Crime," *Emerge Magazine*, June
1997, contained in *The Best of Emerge Magazine*, pp. 17–21.

Newspapers

An assortment of newspapers was consulted to collect primary source
quotes and to verify accounts in other materials. These included the
Anniston Star (Anniston, AL); *Boston Globe* (Boston, MA); *Caroline
Progress* (Bowling Green, VA); *Daily Tar Heel* (Chapel Hill, NC); *Free
Lance-Star* (Fredericksburg, VA); *Los Angeles Times* (Los Angeles, CA);
Montclair Times (Montclair, NJ); *New York Times* (New York, NY);
Progress-Index (Petersburg, VA); and *Seattle Times* (Seattle, WA).

On-site Research

During the snowy week of January 12–19, 2019, I visited the Library
of Virginia (Richmond, VA), the Caroline County Historical Society
(Bowling Green, VA), and the Central Rappahannock Heritage Center
(Fredericksburg, VA) to collect primary source documents.

Websites / Online Articles

Legal Information Institute, "Loving v. Virginia," Cornell Law School:
law.cornell.edu/supremecourt/text/388/1#writing-USSC_
CR_0388_0001_ZO.

Linder, Douglas O. "The Story Behind Loving v. Virginia":
law2.umkc.edu/faculty/projects/ftrials/conlaw/LovingvVirginiaStory.
html.

Oyez, "Loving v. Virginia":oyez.org/cases/1966/395
Listen to the recorded Supreme Court arguments here.

Oyez, "Obergefell v. Hodges": oyez.org/cases/2014/14–556

    Listen to the recorded Supreme Court arguments here.

Virginia Humanities, *Encyclopedia Virginia* (assorted articles and primary

    source documents): encyclopediavirginia.org/.

Interviews

Philip A. Hirschkop, by telephone, August 13, 2018 and July 14, 2019;

    by email, August 14, 2018.

Michael McConnell and Jack Baker, by e-mail, April 30, 2019.

To Find Out More

Besides the youth titles mentioned in the bibliography, younger readers
who want to know more may want to investigate the following:

Brimner, Larry Dane. *Birmingham Sunday*. Honesdale, PA: Calkins Creek,
2010.

Brimner, Larry Dane. *Black and White: The Confrontation between
Reverend Fred L. Shuttlesworth and Eugene "Bull" Connor*. Honesdale,
PA: Calkins Creek, 2011.

Brimner, Larry Dane. *Twelve Days in May: Freedom Ride 1961*.
Honesdale, PA: Calkins Creek, 2017.

Brimner, Larry Dane. *We Are One: The Story of Bayard Rustin*. Honesdale,
PA: Calkins Creek, 2007.

Duncan, Alice Faye, and R. Gregory Christie. *Memphis, Martin, and the
Mountaintop: The Sanitation Strike of 1968*. Honesdale, PA: Calkins
Creek, 2018.

Krull, Kathleen. *A Kids' Guide to America's Bill of Rights*. New York:
Harper, 2015. (Revised Edition).

Levinson, Cynthia, and Sanford Levinson. *Fault Lines in the Constitution: The Framers, Their Fights, and the Flaws that Affect Us Today*. Atlanta: Peachtree Publishers, 2017.

Sanders, Rob, and Jamey Christoph. *Stonewall: A Building. An Uprising. A Revolution*. New York: Random House Children's Books, 2019.

Thomas, Angie. *The Hate U Give*. New York, NY: Balzer & Bray, 2017.

ACKNOWLEDGMENTS

Many people gave freely of their time and expertise to help me with this book. I extend my heartfelt thanks to April C. Armstrong, special collections assistant, Seeley G. Mudd Manuscript Library, Princeton University; Richard John "Jack" Baker, activist; Wayne Brooks, president, Caroline County Historical Society; Nancy Buirski, writer/director, *The Loving Story*; Bernard Collins, past president, Caroline County Historical Society; Philip J. Hirschkop, attorney; Gail Karwoski, author; Abigail Malangone, archivist, John F. Kennedy Presidential Library; Michael McConnell, activist; Robert A. Pratt, professor of history, University of Georgia (Athens); Arlene Z. Rager, volunteer, Central Rappahannock Heritage Center; John Reifenberg, collections manager, Central Rappahannock Heritage Center; Susan Goldman Rubin, writer; Ernest Ryden, for graciously granting permission to use quotes from Hope Ryden's documentary film footage; Dr. Kathy Winings, director, Unification Theological Seminary.

SOURCE NOTES

Front

"Almighty God . . .": Judge Leon M. Bazile, *Encyclopedia Virginia*,
"Primary Resource: opinion, Judge Leon M. Bazile (January
22, 1965)," from original transcript, encyclopediavirginia.org/
Bazile_Leon_M_1890–1967. Website accessed, November 21,
2018. Also, Leon M. Bazile, judge, opinion. "In the Circuit Court of
Caroline County, Commonwealth v. Richard Perry Loving and Mildred
Delores Jeter, Bernard S. Cohen for the Petitioner, Payton Farmer,
Commonwealth Attorney." Transcript, p. 9.

1—July 1958

"I'm his wife.": Mildred Loving, in *The Loving Story*. At "The Crime," 2:45.

"Not here you're . . .": Sheriff Garnett Brooks, as quoted by Mildred
Loving in *The Loving Story*. At "The Crime," 2:47.

"That's no good . . .": Sheriff Garnett Brooks, quoted in Newbeck, p. 11.

"colored—part . . .": "Virginia Ban on Interracial Marriages Goes to
Federal Court This Week," *New York Times*, January 24, 1965.
(Cited, "Virginia Ban.")

"carried us to . . .": Mildred Loving, *The Loving Story*. At "The Crime,"
3:16.

"It never was . . ." and "It [race] doesn't . . .": Richard Loving, quoted in
"The Crime of Being Married," *Life* magazine, March 18, 1966, p.
88. (Cited, "The Crime of Being Married.")

"hillbilly music": Mildred Loving, quoted in "Wife Recalls Victory in Battle to Overturn Ban on Interracial Marriage," by Ann Gearan, *Los Angeles Times*, November 8, 1962. (Cited, "Wife Recalls.")

"When we first . . .": Mildred Loving, *The Loving Story*. At "Home," 00:24.

"You've got to . . .": Oscar Hammerstein II and Richard Rogers, "You've Got to be Carefully Taught," *South Pacific*, 1949 (Broadway premier).

"Intermarriage . . .": David C. Jones, quoted in "'South Pacific' Lyric Branded Race Propaganda in Georgia," the *Daily Tar Heel* (Chapel Hill, NC), March 4, 1953.

"pure blood lines . . .": Ibid.

"I didn't know . . ." and "We were just . . .": Mildred Loving, quoted in "Wife Recalls."

"We weren't out . . .": Ibid.

"But we had . . .": Ibid.

"did go out . . .": "State of Virginia, County of Caroline, To-Wit: Commonwealth Warrant: Mildred Jeter," July 11, 1958.

"as man and . . .": Ibid.

"Richard Perry Loving . . .": Gladys Livermon. "Commonwealth of Virginia, County of Caroline, To-Wit, in the Circuit Court of Said County. Grand Jury Indictment for a Felony." Transcript.

"The grand jury . . .": "Joseph Buck Martin Indicted Mon. in Slaying of Wife, August 11," the *Caroline Progress*, October 16, 1958.

"at one year . . .": Judge Leon M. Bazile, "Commonwealth vs. Richard Perry Loving and Mildred Delores Jeter: Indictment for a Felony," opinion, January 6, 1959.

"upon the provision . . .": Ibid.

2—Banishment

"the children didn't . . .": Mildred Loving, *The Loving Story*. At "Exile,"
3:54.

"That Easter . . .": Mildred Loving, *The Loving Story*. At "Exile," 7:44.

"The way I . . .": Mildred Loving, *The Loving Story*. At "Exile," 7:35.

"We left there . . .": Richard Loving, The *Loving Story*. At "Exile," 7:51.

"In Washington . . .": Mildred Loving, *The Loving Story*. At "Exile," 8:06.

"When they wanted . . .": Peggy Loving, *The Loving Story*. At "Exile,"
1:48.

"I wasn't involved . . .": Mildred Loving, *The Loving Story*. At "Exile,"
5:22.

"That was the straw . . .": Mildred Loving, *The Loving Story*. At "Exile,"
4:27.

"I was so . . . ": Mildred Loving, *The Loving Story*. At "Exile," 4:36.

"there wasn't . . .": Mildred Loving, *The Loving Story*. At "Exile," 6:36.

"Dear Sir: . . ." and "5 yrs. ago . . .": Mildred Loving, letter to the
American Civil Liberties Union, dated June 20, 1963.

"to the Attorney . . . ": Ibid.

3—The Case

"relics of slavery . . .": Bernard Cohen, *The Loving Story*, At "The
Climate," 4:28.

"Marriage . . .": Bernard Cohen, *The Loving Story*. At "The Climate," 4:39.

"an unbelievable challenge . . .": Bernard Cohen, *The Loving Story*. At
"The Climate," 6:21.

"still in the . . .": Wallenstein, Peter. *Race, Sex, and the Freedom to Marry:
Loving v. Virginia*. Lawrence, Kansas: University Press of Kansas,
2014, p. 101. (Cited, *Race, Sex*.)

"sentence constitutes cruel . . ." and "exceeds the reasonable . . .":
    Bernard Cohen, writing in Circuit Court of the County of Caroline,
    State of Virginia, "Motion to Vacate Judgment and Set Aside
    Sentence," transcript, held at Central Rappahannock Heritage Center,
    Fredericksburg, VA, paragraphs A and B, p. 1. (Cited, "Motion to
    Vacate.")

"sentence constitutes banishment . . .": Ibid., paragraph C.

"unconstitutional on its . . .": Ibid., paragraph D.

"such sentence has . . .": Ibid., paragraph F, p. 2.

"Can they really . . .": Mildred Loving, letter to Bernard Cohen, dated
    July 6, 1964, quoted in *Race, Sex*, p. 103.

"a preliminary injunction . . .": Bernard Cohen and Philip Hirschkop,
    "In the United States District Court for the Eastern District of Virginia,
    Richmond District." Undated. (Makes reference to Judge John D.
    Butzner for identification.)

"decide upon the . . .": Ibid. (Makes reference to Constitutionality for
    identification.)

"solely for the . . .": *Race, Sex*, p. 105.

"irreparable injury": Philip Hirschkop, *The Loving Story*. At "The Case," 7:28.

"by citing cases . . .": Newbeck, p. 142.

"each one of them . . ." Judge Leon M. Bazile, opinion, "In the Circuit
    Court of Caroline County, Commonwealth v. Richard Perry Loving
    and Mildred Delores Jeter, Bernard S. Cohen for the Petitioner, Peyton
    Farmer, Commonwealth Attorney." Transcript (undated), p. 8. (Cited
    "Bazile Opinion.")

"belongs to the . . .": Ibid., p. 5.

"unlawful and absolutely void": Ibid., p. 9.

"when Judge Bazile . . .": Philip Hirschkop, the *Loving Story*. At "The Case," 2:18.

"Almighty God created . . .": "Bazile Opinion," p. 9.

"marriage between a . . .": "Bazile Opinion," p. 9.

"All we want . . .": Mildred Loving, quoted in "Virginia Ban."

"They said I . . ." and "leaving home . . .": Richard Loving, quoted in "Virginia Ban."

"The Constitution of Virginia . . .": "Virginia: In the Circuit Court of Caroline County Commonwealth of Virginia vs. Richard Perry Loving and Mildred Delores Jeter, Criminal No. 928 & 929. Notice of Appeal and Assignment of Error." Transcript, p. 1.

"reasonable limits": Ibid., p. 2.

"If the right . . .": "Perez v. Sharp, 32 Cal.2d 711," October 1, 1948. Transcript. (scocal.stanford.edu/opinion/perez-v-sharp-26107) Accessed 3/26/2019.

"fully investigated . . .": Justice Harry L. Carrico, opinion, "Richard Perry Loving, et al. v. Record No. 6163 Commonwealth of Virginia," March 7, 1966, p. 3.

"The purpose which . . ." and "not again cohabit . . .": Ibid., p. 13.

"We have thought . . .": Richard Loving, quoted in "The Crime of Being Married," p. 91.

4—April 10, 1967

"This is strictly . . .": Philip Hirschkop, *The Loving Story*. At "The Court," 1:57.

"don't want to . . .": Ibid. At "The Court," 2:22.

Naim v. Naim: Han Say Naim is referred to as "Ham Say Naim" in some
   sources. The spelling used here is from the Supreme Court of Virginia,
   Record No. 4368, June 13, 1955.

"I probably wouldn't . . .": Richard Loving, *The Loving Story*. At "The
   Court," 7:49.

"Mr. Chief Justice . . .": Philip Hirschkop, quoted in Peter Irons and
   Stephanie Guitton, editors, *May It Please the Court: The Most
   Significant Oral Arguments Made before the Supreme Court since
   1955*; New York, NY: The New Press, 1993, p. 279. Transcript.
   (Cited "May It Please.")

"the racial integrity . . .": Ibid., p. 280.

"May the state . . .": Ibid.

"Almighty God": Judge Leon M. Bazile, "Bazile Opinion," p. 9.

"It's a fundamentally . . .": Philip Hirschkop, *May It Please*, p. 280.

"to keep the slaves . . .": Ibid., p. 280.

"rob the Negro race . . .": Ibid., p. 281.

"it would have . . .": Bernard Cohen, *May It Please*, p. 285.

"meant to include . . .": Ibid.

"to wake up in . . .": Ibid.

"that should they . . .": Ibid.

"No one can . . .": Ibid.

"Your Honor . . .": Bernard Cohen, Oyez.org, "Loving v. Virginia,"
   oral argument, April 10, 1967. Recording/Transcript. Accessed
   4/3/2019.

"This question has . . .": Ibid.

"These statutes in . . .": Robert D. McIlwaine III, Oyez.org, "Loving v.
   Virginia," oral argument, April 10, 1967. Recording/Transcript.
   Accessed 4/3/2019.

"this Court under . . .": Ibid.

"sociological, psychological evils . . .": Ibid.

"that society is . . ." and "that it has . . .": Ibid.

"definitive book . . .": Ibid.

"have a rebellious . . .": Robert D. McIlwaine III, *May It Please*, p. 283.

"You don't know . . .": Justice Potter Stewart, Oyez.org, "Loving
   v. Virginia," oral arguments, April 10, 1967. Recording/
   Transcript. Accessed 4/3/2019. Quote is attributed to Justice
   Byron White in *May It Please*, but confirmed as Potter Stewart at
   EncyclopediaVirginia.org.

"whites would be . . .": Chief Justice Earl Warren, Oyez.org, "Loving v.
   Virginia," oral argument, April 10, 1967. Recording/Transcript.

"to invalidate . . .": Bernard Cohen, Oyez.org, "Loving v. Virginia," oral
   argument, April 10, 1967. Recording/Transcript.

"We conclude . . .": Chief Justice Earl Warren, opinion. Legal Information
   Institute, Cornell Law School, *Loving v. Virginia*. law.cornell.edu/
   supremecourt/text/388/1#writing-USSC_CR_0388_0001_ZO.
   Accessed 4/5/2019.

"that marriage is . . .": Ibid.

"Marriage is one . . .": Chief Justice Earl Warren, *May It Please*, pp.
   288–289.

5—After *Loving*

"Give me your . . .": Emma Lazarus, "The New Colossus," poets.org,
   poets.org/poetsorg/poem/new-colossus. Accessed 4/7/2019.

"The Massachusetts Constitution . . .": Chief Justice Margaret H. Marshall,
   opinion, "Same-Sex Marriage; Excerpts from the Massachusetts
   Ruling," the *New York Times*, November 19, 2003.

"Recognizing the right . . .": Ibid.

"The right to marry . . .": Justice Anthony Kennedy, majority opinion, "Obergefell, et al., v. Hodges, Director, Ohio Department of Health, et al.," transcript, June 26, 2015, p. 22.

"far from seeking . . .": Ibid., p. 4.

"I believe all . . .": Mildred Loving, quoted in Judith E. Schaeffer, "Marriage Equality Battle Based on Local Case," the *Free Lance-Star* (Fredericksburg, VA), undated; also, Judith E. Schaeffer, guest columnist, "Schaeffer: The Power of Loving," the *Virginian-Pilot*, pilotonline.com, February 15, 2014.

"No union is more . . .": Justice Anthony Kennedy, majority opinion, "Obergefell, et al. v. Hodges, Director, Ohio Department of Health, et al.," June 26, 2015.

Author's Note

"from the Latin . . .": David G. Croly, *Miscegenation: The Theory of the Blending of the Races, applied to The American White Man and Negro*, London, England: FB&c Ltd., 2018, p. ii. Forgotten Books edition. (Cited, Miscegenation.)

"when the President . . .": Miscegenation, 49.

"The Republican party . . .": Ibid.

"The dark races . . .": Miscegenation, p. 17.

"unlawful for any . . .": *Encyclopedia Virginia*, "Primary Resource: Preservation of Racial Integrity (1924)," paragraph 5, from original transcript. encyclopediavirginia.org/preservation_of_Racial_Integrity_1924. Accessed 2/17/2019.

"one drop rule": *Encyclopedia Virginia*, "Racial Integrity Laws (1924–1930)," contributed by Brendan Wolfe, encyclopediavirginia. org/Racial_Integrity_Laws_of_the_1920s. Accessed 2/17/2019.

"I know during . . ." and "But she was . . .": Mark Loving, quoted in Curt Autry, "Grandson Say 'Loving' Movie Gets One Key Point Wrong," NBC-12 On Your Side, November 3, 2016, updated August 12. nbc12.com/story/33617723/grandson-say-loving-movie-gets-one-key-point-wrong/ Accessed 11/18/2018.

"true, to the . . .": Application for License, image. Ibid.

"part negro, & . . .": Mildred Loving, letter to the American Civil Liberties Union, June 20, 1963. Courtesy of Philip Hirschkop.

"The marriage is . . . ": Gwendolyn Smith, "The First Same-sex Marriage in the U.S. Now Officially Happened in 1971," *LGBTQ Nation*, February 26, 2019 (lgbtqnation.com/2019/02/first-sex-marriage-u-s-now-officially-happened-1971/); and Nancy Dillon, "Same-sex Couple Who Got Marriage License in 1971 Celebrate Long-awaited Social Security Letter Validating 47-Year Union," *New York Daily News*, March 7, 2019 (nydailynews.com/news/ny-news-same-sex-couple-minnesota-ss-letter-validating-marriage-20190307-story.html).

INDEX

Page numbers in **boldface** refer to images and/or captions.

71, 74, 76, 77, **78**, **79**, 80,
83
avoids interracial marriage,
34, 58
rules against marriage bans,
67

V

Virginia (Commonwealth of), **6**, 9,
10, **11**, **13**, 14, 16, **17**, 18,
19, **20**, **22–23**, 24, 25, 26,
27, 34, 35, 39, 40, 41, 43,
44, **45**, 46, **48–49**, 50, 51,
52, 58, 59, 60, 61, **62–63**,
64, 65, 66, 67, 71, **79**, 82,
83, 85
Virginia Constitution, 38, 46
Voting Rights Act of, 1965, 52,
54–55

W

Wakeman, George, 81
Warren, Chief Justice Earl, 60, 61,
66, 67
Loving opinion, 67
Washington, DC (District of
Columbia), 16, **17**, 18, 25,
26, 27, 30, **31**, 35, 39, 41,
48–49, 76, **79**
West Virginia, 44

Windsor, Edith, 76, **78**
bill from Internal Revenue
Service, 76
World War II, 14
Wyoming, 44

Z

Zabel, William D., 59, 60

PICTURE CREDITS

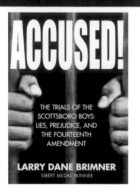

Blacklisted!: Hollywood, the Cold War, and the First Amendment

A *Kirkus Reviews* Best Children's Book
★*Booklist*, STARRED REVIEW
★*Kirkus Reviews*, STARRED REVIEW
★*School Library Journal*, STARRED REVIEW
★*Shelf Awareness*, STARRED REVIEW

Strike! The Farm Workers' Fight for Their Rights

Notable Books for a Global Society Book Award
Orbis Pictus Award Recommended Book
VOYA's Perfect 10
★*Booklist*, STARRED REVIEW
★*Kirkus Reviews*, STARRED REVIEW
★*School Library Journal*, STARRED REVIEW

Twelve Days in May: Freedom Ride 1961

Sibert Medal Winner
ALSC Notable Children's Book
Carter G. Woodson Book Award
Booklist Editors' Choice
A Chicago Public Library Best of the Best Book
★*Booklist*, STARRED REVIEW
★*School Library Journal*, STARRED REVIEW

We Are One: The Story of Bayard Rustin

Jane Addams Book Award for Older Children
Norman A. Sugarman Children's Biography Award
New York Public Library Books for the Teen Age
★*School Library Connection*, STARRED REVIEW
★*School Library Journal*, STARRED REVIEW

Text Permission (page 14)
You've Got To Be Carefully Taught
from SOUTH PACIFIC
Lyrics by Oscar Hammerstein II
Music by Richard Rodgers
Copyright (c) 1949 by Richard Rodgers and Oscar Hammerstein II
Copyright Renewed
Williamson Music, a Division of Rodgers & Hammerstein: an Imagem Company, owner of publication and allied rights throughout the world
International Copyright Secured All Rights Reserved
Reprinted by Permission of Hal Leonard LLC

Calkins Creek
An imprint of Boyds Mills & Kane, a division of Astra Publishing House
calkinscreekbooks.com
Printed in China

ISBN: 978-1-62979-751-9 (hc)
eISBN: 978-1-63592-450-3
Library of Congress Control Number: 2019953795

First edition
10 9 8 7 6 5 4 3 2 1

Design by Barbara Grzeslo
The text is set in Futura.
The titles are set in Impact.